MODULE 1: COURSE INTRODUCTION

This page intentionally left blank.

COURSE INTRODUCTION

Visual 1.1

Key Points

Welcome to the Multihazard Planning for Childcare course.

COURSE INTRODUCTION

Visual 1.2

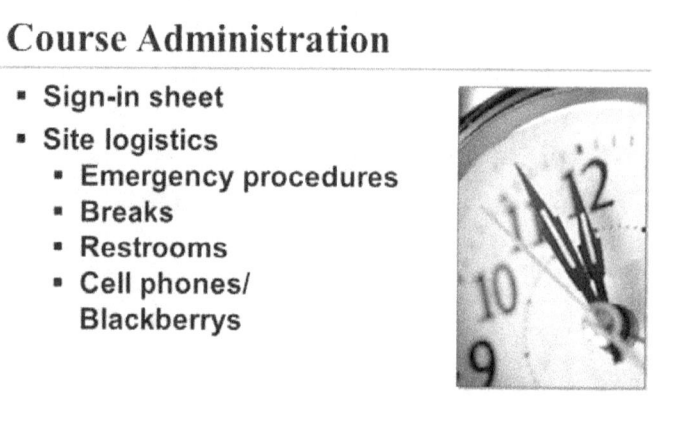

Key Points

The visual explains the ground rules on breaks and cell phones.

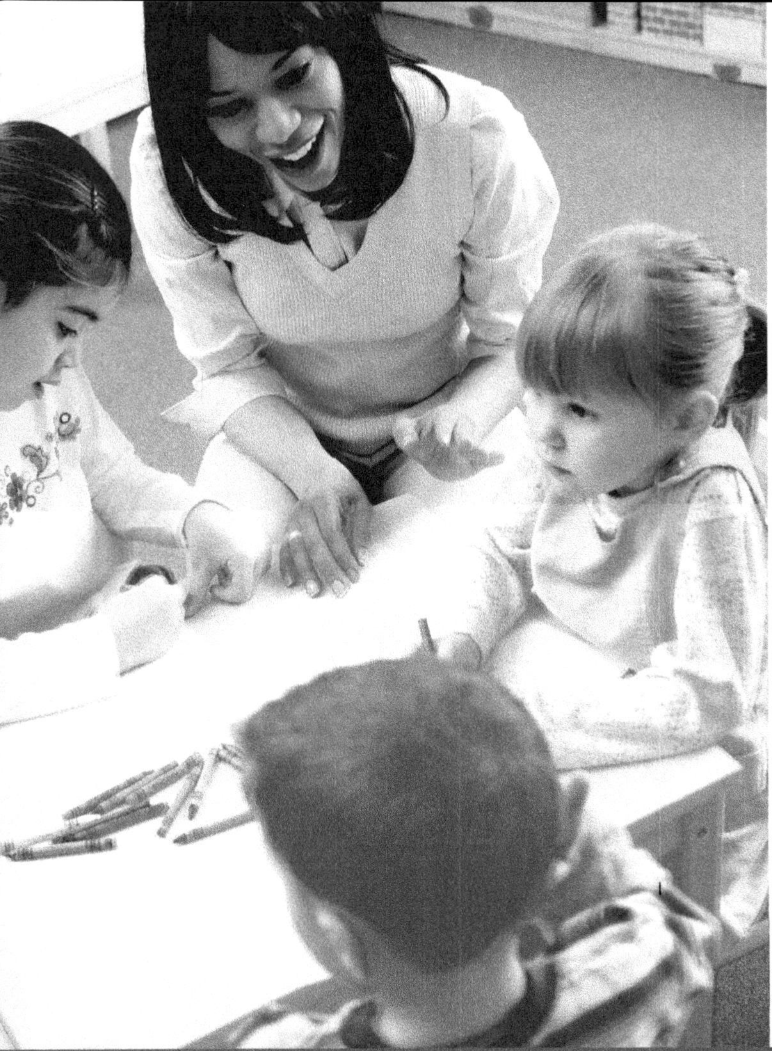

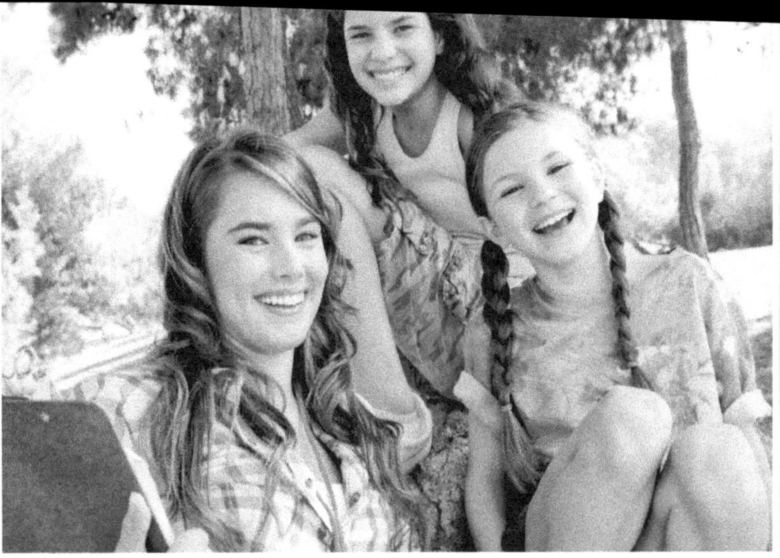

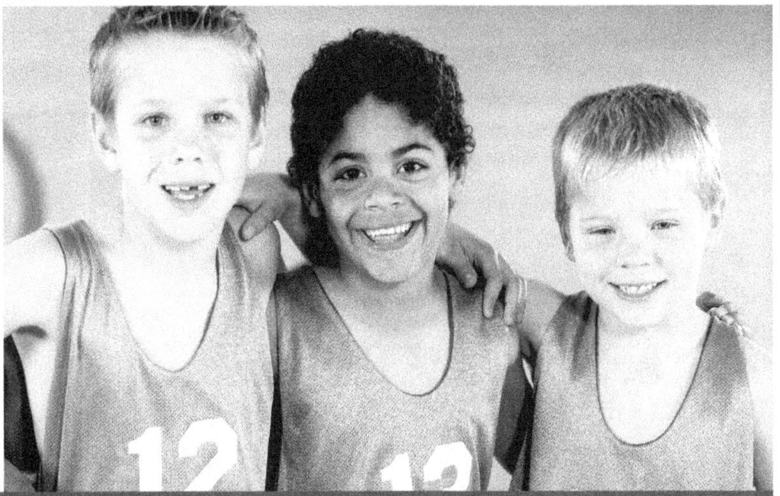

IS-36:
Multihazard Planning for Childcare

Student Manual

February 2012

COURSE INTRODUCTION

Visual 1.3

Course Goal

Provide childcare providers with the knowledge and tools to:

- Analyze the hazards and threats at the site.
- Develop a plan to address these hazards and threats.
- Implement processes to update and practice the emergency plan.

FEMA

Visual 1.3
IS-36 Multihazard Planning for Childcare

Key Points

The goal of this course is to provide childcare providers, of all sizes and with responsibility for children of all ages, with the knowledge and tools to analyze the hazards and threats at the site, to develop a plan to address these hazards and threats, and to implement processes to update and practice the emergency plan.

COURSE INTRODUCTION

Visual 1.4

Course Objectives (1 of 2)

- Describe why it is important to be prepared.
- Identify hazards and threats that impact your childcare site.
- Describe how to prevent or mitigate the impact of likely and high-consequence hazards and threats.
- Describe procedures for when an emergency occurs.
- Identify how your childcare site will recover from an emergency.

FEMA
Visual 1.4
IS-36 Multihazard Planning for Childcare

Key Points

By the end of this course, you should be able to:

- Describe why it is important to be prepared.
- Identify hazards and threats that impact your childcare site.
- Describe how to prevent or mitigate the impact of likely and high-consequence hazards and threats.
- Describe procedures for when an emergency occurs.
- Identify how your childcare site will recover from an emergency.

COURSE INTRODUCTION

Visual 1.5

Course Objectives (2 of 2)

- Describe how to develop and maintain your plan.
- Describe how you will communicate, train, and practice your preparedness procedures.
- Identify the emergency preparedness information you will share with your community.
- Describe when to update your plan.

FEMA
Visual 1.5
IS-36 Multihazard Planning for Childcare

Key Points

By the end of this course, you should be able to:

- Describe how to develop and maintain your plan.
- Describe how you will communicate, train, and practice your preparedness procedures.
- Identify the emergency preparedness information you will share with your community.
- Describe when to update your plan.

THE IMPORTANCE OF PREPAREDNESS

Visual 1.6

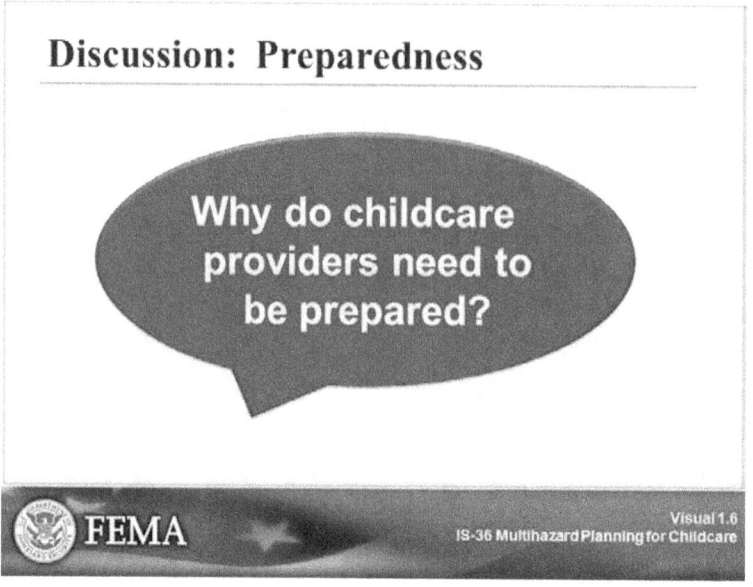

Key Points

Why do childcare providers need to be prepared?

Nearly two-thirds of children under the age of 6 are cared for by someone other than their working parents. This means that children spend most of their awake time away from home in places like home childcare sites, childcare facilities, nursery schools, camps, Scouts, sports programs, faith-based programs, and after-school programs.

As someone who is taking care of these children, you need to be ready to keep them safe.

THE IMPORTANCE OF PREPAREDNESS

Visual 1.7

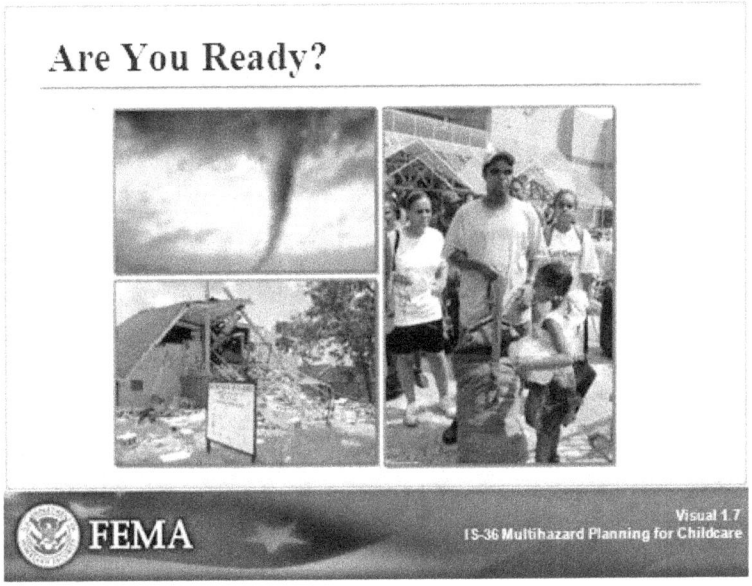

Key Points

As a childcare provider, you are responsible for one of the most vulnerable populations – children. Caring for children is serious business, and their safety is your number one priority.

News headlines are full of examples illustrating why you need to be prepared. Some stories we know with just the mention of a name – 9/11, Oklahoma City, Katrina. But others, less publicized, are just as devastating. For example:

- A fire breaks out in a home childcare facility, and two children perish in the fire.
- While on a hike with his troop, a Boy Scout dies of heat stroke.
- A childcare facility takes a direct hit from a powerful tornado.

Consider this scenario: A gas line is hit in front of a childcare center. Firefighters praise the center's evacuation process and attribute the successful evacuation to the center having a comprehensive plan and practicing it.

It is not a matter of if something will happen, but when.

THE IMPORTANCE OF PREPAREDNESS

Visual 1.8

What Can You Do?

Being prepared helps you to:
- Save lives.
- Prevent incidents from happening.
- Minimize injury.
- Decrease damage to your property.
- Reduce fear and the emotional impact of an incident.
- Recover more quickly.

FEMA

Visual 1.8
IS-36 Multihazard Planning for Childcare

Key Points

Being prepared helps you to:

- Save lives—the lives of the children in your care and your staff, as well as your own life.
- Prevent incidents from happening.
- Minimize injury.
- Decrease damage to your property.
- Reduce fear and the emotional impact of an incident.
- Recover more quickly.

THE IMPORTANCE OF PREPAREDNESS

Visual 1.9

What Do Parents Expect?

Parents expect you to:

- Have a plan for emergencies.
- Be able to safely evacuate.
- Notify them when something happens.
- Care for their children.
- Teach their children what to do during an emergency.
- Have sufficient supplies.
- Have relationships with emergency management officials and first responders.

FEMA

Visual 1.9
IS-36 Multihazard Planning for Childcare

Key Points

An important aspect of being prepared is meeting parents' expectations that you will keep their children safe. Parents want to know that their child's safety is a priority at all times. Parents expect you to:

- Have a plan for emergencies.
- Be able to safely evacuate the children in your care when necessary.
- Notify them when something happens.
- Care for their children if they cannot get to them.
- Teach their children what to do during an emergency.
- Have supplies to meet their children's needs.
- Have relationships with emergency management officials and first responders before something happens.

THE IMPORTANCE OF PREPAREDNESS

Visual 1.10

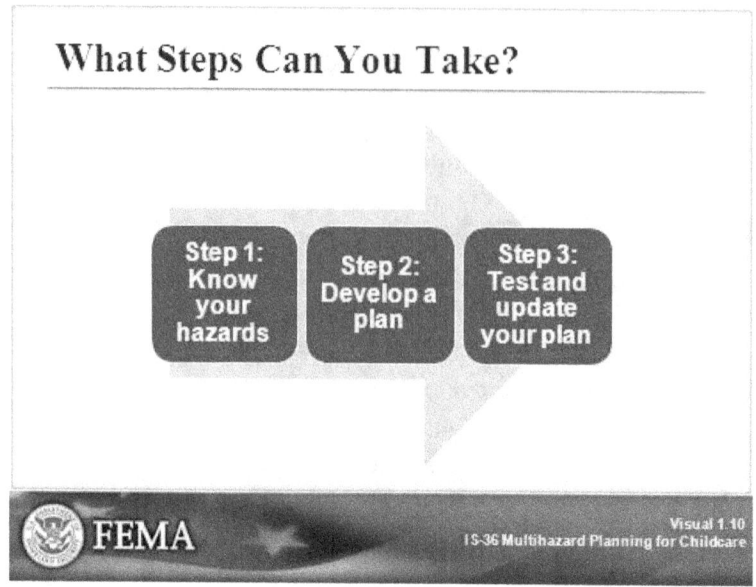

Key Points

Taking some simple steps to be prepared will help you meet parents' expectations, and will also give you confidence that you can prevent incidents or lessen the impact of incidents and act appropriately when something happens.

This course presents a process of three steps to get you ready.

- Step 1: Know your hazards.
- Step 2: Develop a plan.
- Step 3: Test and update your plan.

THE IMPORTANCE OF PREPAREDNESS

Visual 1.11

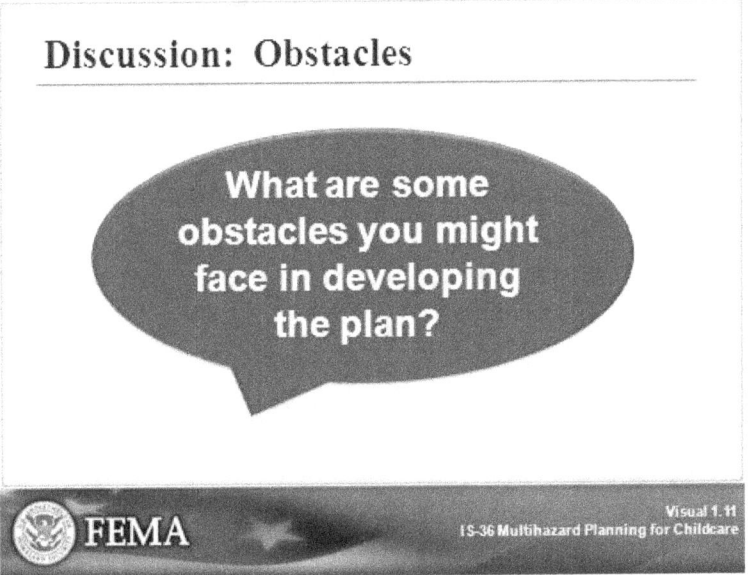

Key Points

Your childcare site has identified the need to develop a plan to prepare for emergencies. What are some obstacles (e.g., time, resources, expertise) you might face in developing the plan?

THE IMPORTANCE OF PREPAREDNESS

Visual 1.12

Obstacles to Planning

- Getting the right people involved
- Finding time to conduct planning.
- Being overwhelmed by possible hazards and threats.
- Lacking contacts in the emergency field.

FEMA

Visual 1.12
IS-36 Multihazard Planning for Childcare

Key Points

Some obstacles to planning may include:

- **Getting the right people involved.** You may encounter obstacles to getting stakeholders to participate in the planning process. Making sure you have input from people with diverse expertise is important, so be persistent.

- **Finding time to conduct planning.** You are busy taking care of children, so you may have a hard time determining when you can plan for emergencies. Remember that planning is necessary for one very important reason: you are responsible for the safety of the children in your care. Identify time for planning and stick to it. Include children, staff, and parents in planning and practice, where appropriate.

- **Being overwhelmed by possible hazards and threats.** It can be overwhelming and scary to think about all the hazards and threats that you may face, but because of the magnitude of your responsibility to care for children, you must be prepared. Consider working with others to help you manage the task—staff, parents, other childcare sites, and emergency personnel.

- **Lacking contacts in the emergency field.** Now is the perfect time to reach out to police, fire, emergency medical services, and your local emergency manager. They can provide you valuable assistance and lessen some of the other obstacles to planning.

MODULE SUMMARY

Visual 1.13

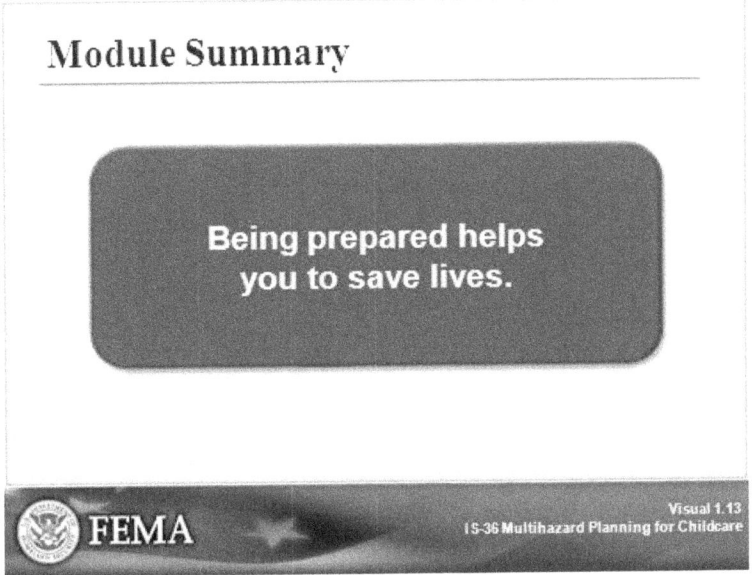

Key Points

This module reviewed the importance of preparedness in a childcare facility.

The next module will describe common hazards, and steps you can take to reduce the risks of these hazards.

This page intentionally left blank.

MODULE 2: KNOWING YOUR HAZARDS

This page intentionally left blank.

MODULE INTRODUCTION

Visual 2.1

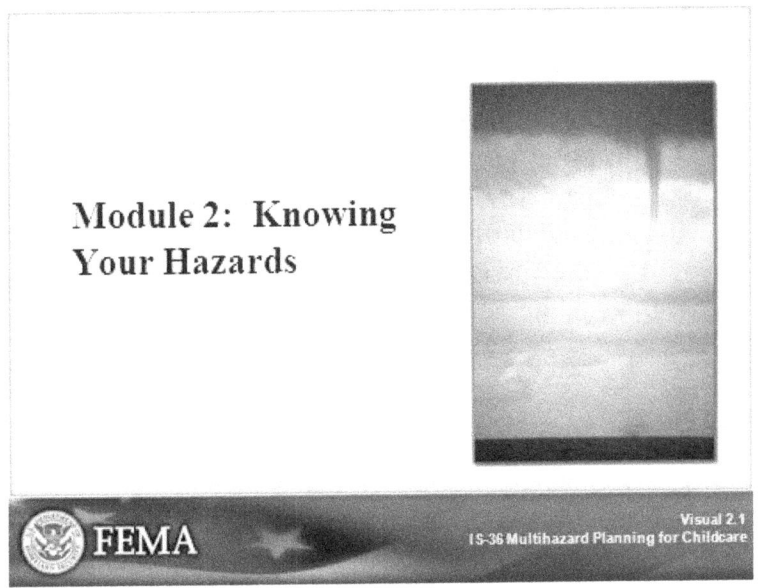

Key Points

This module reviews different hazards and threats to help you identify which hazards to focus on, and gives you strategies to:

- Prevent the hazard, or
- Minimize the hazard's impact, and
- Prepare for the hazard.

MODULE INTRODUCTION

Visual 2.2

Module Objectives

- Identify hazards and threats that impact your childcare site.
- Describe how to prevent or mitigate the impact of likely and high-consequence hazards and threats.

FEMA

Visual 2.2
IS-36 Multihazard Planning for Childcare

Key Points

By the end of this module, you should be able to:

- Identify hazards and threats that impact your childcare site.
- Describe how to prevent or mitigate the impact of likely and high-consequence hazards and threats.

MODULE INTRODUCTION

Visual 2.3

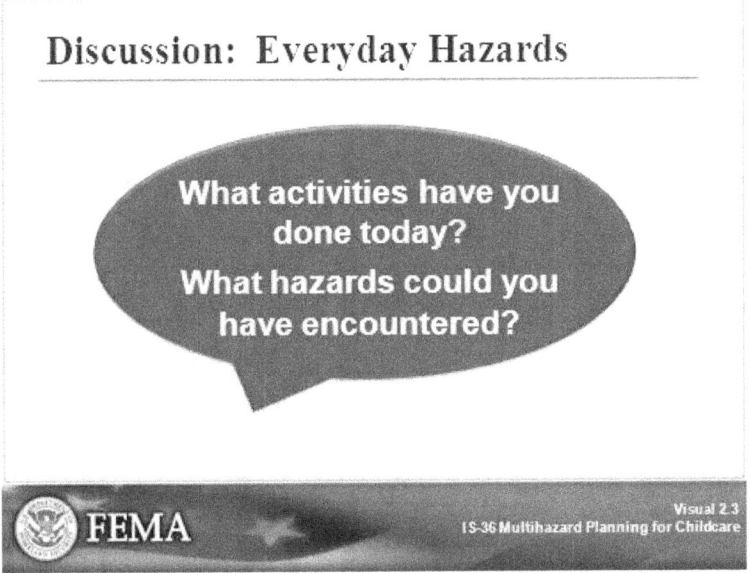

Key Points

What activities have you done today?

What hazards could you have encountered?

IDENTIFYING HAZARDS

Visual 2.4

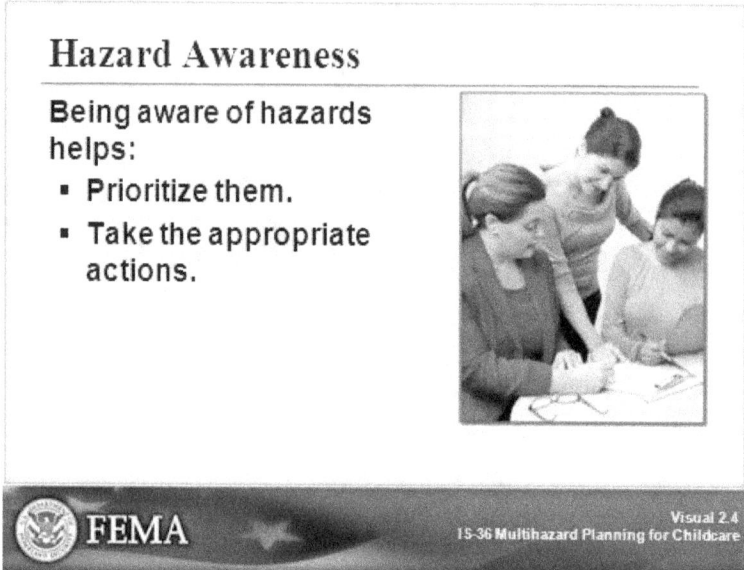

Key Points

Focusing on all the hazards you might encounter can be overwhelming. Dwelling on all the everyday hazards that surround us might make it difficult to get out of bed! Nonetheless, it is necessary to be aware of hazards to develop strategies to prevent them, prepare for them, and/or minimize their impact.

Being aware of hazards helps you prioritize them and take the appropriate actions. For example, driving your car is dangerous, but you wear your seatbelt to minimize injury and you purchase insurance to help you recover from an accident.

IDENTIFYING HAZARDS

Visual 2.5

Who Can Help Identify Hazards

- Local/county emergency manager
- Parents
- First responders
- Local schools and school district
- State department of health
- Childcare site insurance carrier
- Utility company personnel
- Local business and industry personnel
- Childcare organizations

FEMA

Visual 2.5
IS-36 Multihazard Planning for Childcare

Key Points

An important part of being aware of your hazards is including the whole community in the identification process. Include community members in all of your preparedness efforts, because they have access to information or subject-matter expertise about threats, hazards, and emergency procedures. People who will bring valuable information to your planning include:

- Your **local/county emergency manager** has historical information about hazards and threats in your community.
- **Parents** can provide expertise based on their experiences and professional knowledge (e.g., in the medical field, in the construction business), or may have had response training.
- **First responders** (e.g., fire marshal, law enforcement) can check your facility for safety hazards and identify vulnerabilities.
- **Local schools and the local school district** can provide information about their planning efforts.
- Your **State department of health** may have requirements for emergency planning and may be able to provide guidance and training.
- Your **childcare site insurance carrier** can provide information about potential risk reduction measures and procedures for claims.
- **Utility company personnel** can identify how to shut off utilities and who to contact with issues or questions.
- **Local business and industry personnel** can provide expertise based on their knowledge and areas of expertise.

IDENTIFYING HAZARDS

Visual 2.5, continued

- **Childcare organizations** can provide best practices information around preparedness for childcare sites. Childcare resource and referral agencies have resources to help sites with many aspects of running a childcare facility including emergency preparedness.

  The Web site for the National Association of Child Care Resource & Referral Agencies has links to local resources: www.naccrra.org

An added benefit to including the community in your planning process is an increased awareness of the existence of your site, enabling you to be alerted to external emergency situations (for example, if there is a hazardous materials spill near your site).

IDENTIFYING HAZARDS

Visual 2.6

Hazards: Fire

Fires:
- Are the most common of all business disasters.
- Can spread quickly and are dangerous.
- In childcare centers are usually started by a cooking accident.

FEMA

Visual 2.6
IS-36 Multihazard Planning for Childcare

Key Points

Fire is the most common of business disasters.

Below are some sobering facts about fire:

- More than 4,000 Americans die and more than 20,000 are injured by fire each year.
- Fires can spread quickly and are dangerous not only because of the flames but also the heat, smoke, and poisonous gases emitted.
- Asphyxiation is the leading cause of fire-related deaths.
- Cooking is the leading cause of fires in childcare centers.
- It is difficult for young children to escape from fire because they lack the motor skills and mental capabilities needed and may be unable to awake from a sound sleep.

IDENTIFYING HAZARDS

Visual 2.7

Fire Protection

- Have an evacuation plan.
- Practice your plan and make sure everyone can get out of each room.
- Install, test, and clean smoke alarms.
- Schedule visits from the fire department for fire safety information.

FEMA
Visual 2.7
IS-36 Multihazard Planning for Childcare

Key Points

Here are some general steps to protect yourself and the children in your care from the hazards of fire:

- Have an evacuation plan.
- Practice your plan and make sure everyone can get out of each room.
  - Are windows painted or nailed shut?
  - Do you have escape ladders?
  - Can you evacuate children who cannot evacuate on their own?
- Install, test, and clean smoke alarms.
- Schedule visits from the fire department for fire safety information.

Use the job aid on the following page to assess the risk level of fire at your childcare site, and to identify steps you can take to minimize your risk and prepare your site.

Job Aid: Hazard Identification: Fire

Identify Hazard/Threat Risk Level (circle one): *None, Low, Moderate, or High*	
✓ **Steps to reduce my risk:**	**Comments**

☐   Have properly working smoke detectors.
  • Place smoke detectors on every level of your facility and, if possible, in every sleeping area.
  • Test and clean smoke detectors once a month.
  • Replace batteries in your smoke detectors at least once a year. If the alarm chirps, replace the battery immediately.
☐   Have heating, cooling, gas, and electrical systems checked regularly.
☐   Use fire-resistant materials.
☐   Install carbon monoxide detectors.
☐   Install sprinklers, if possible.
☐   Install fire extinguishers in each room and check regularly (i.e., charge levels, mounted securely, within easy reach, staff and volunteers know how to use).
☐   Have a plan to evacuate infants and toddlers.
☐   Have the fire marshal visit the facility regularly. (Ask about fire codes, regulations, and training for children and staff.)
☐   Keep portable heaters at least 3 feet away from things that can burn – paper, curtains, furniture, bedding, clothing, etc. Ensure they are turned off when adults are not in the room.
☐   Keep matches and lighters up high and, if possible, in a locked cabinet.
☐   Train on STOP, DROP, and ROLL and evacuation procedures.
☐   Check for overloaded outlets.
☐   Have a site diagram.
☐   Clear exits and ensure there are two exits for evacuation, clearly marked.
  • All windows open.
  • Doors are unobstructed.
  • Escape ladders are available for higher floors.
☐   Have a designated meeting area.
☐   Cut back bushes and trees.
☐ Ensure street address is clearly visible.	

IDENTIFYING HAZARDS

Visual 2.8

Activity

Instructions: Working as a team . . .

1. Create a list of three ways you might evacuate several children at one time, including infants, toddlers, and children with access and functional needs.

2. Record your list on chart paper.

3. Select a spokesperson and be prepared to present your list in 5 minutes.

FEMA

Visual 2.8
IS-36 Multihazard Planning for Childcare

Key Points

Purpose: This activity will give you the opportunity to identify strategies for evacuating children.

Instructions: Working in teams . . .

1. Create a list of three ways you might evacuate several children at one time, including infants, toddlers, and children with access and functional needs.
2. Record your list on chart paper.
3. Select a spokesperson and be prepared to present your list in 5 minutes.

IDENTIFYING HAZARDS

Visual 2.9

Key Points

Let's now look at what you can do to address risks related to general safety.

General safety includes childproofing. For sites with young children, follow the American Academy of Pediatrics process of taking a "child's-eye view" survey, going from room to room and addressing the hazards at the level of a curious toddler.

Ensure that the safety measures you take are in accordance with local/State childcare licensing requirements.

Use the job aid on the following page to assess the general safety at your childcare site and to identify steps you can take to minimize your risk and prepare your site.

Job Aid: Hazard Identification: General Safety

Identify Hazard/Threat Risk Level (circle one): _None, Low, Moderate, or High_		
✓	**Steps to reduce my risk:**	**Comments**
☐	Childproof the facility. • Protect electrical outlets. • Remove access to electrical cords. • Place safety locks on cabinets. • Place door knob covers on doors. • Place safety gates at top and bottom of stairs. • Ensure window blind strings do not have loops. • Secure tall furniture to walls. • Lock up cleaning products. • Lock medicines in high cabinets. • Place locks on toilets. • Place guards on windows. • Place corner and edge bumpers on sharp edges of furniture. • Place houseplants out of reach of children. • Remove choking hazards. • Keep cribs away from draperies, blinds, and electrical cords.	
☐	Ensure children cannot access water features (e.g., ponds, fountains, pools).	
☐	Ensure trash is not accessible to children.	
☐	Remove broken or unsafe play equipment.	
☐	Designate any unsafe areas as off-limits to children.	
☐	Follow established standards for the care of infants with respect to sudden infant death syndrome (SIDS).	

IDENTIFYING HAZARDS

Visual 2.10

Hazards: Hazardous Materials

Make sure hazardous materials are:

- Clearly marked.
- Kept in their original containers.
- Stored out of children's reach.

FEMA

Visual 2.10
IS-36 Multihazard Planning for Childcare

Key Points

Let's now look at what you can do to address risks related to hazardous materials in and around your childcare site.

Hazardous materials can be found in all homes and businesses and include cleaning products, pesticides, paint supplies, and lawn and garden products. Make sure hazardous materials are clearly marked, kept in their original containers, and stored out of children's reach. Explosions are an important risk associated with having hazardous materials at your site.

Use the job aid on the following page to assess the risk level of hazardous materials and to identify steps you can take to minimize your risk and prepare your site.

Job Aid: Hazard Identification: Hazardous Materials

Identify Hazard/Threat Risk Level (circle one): None, Low, Moderate, or High		
✓ **Steps to reduce my risk:**		**Comments**
☐	Lock up chemicals, poisonous/toxic items, medicines, and flammable items.	
☐	Dispose of hazardous materials correctly.	
☐	Keep products containing hazardous materials in their original containers. Do not remove labels. Do not store hazardous materials in food containers.	
☐	Know who to call when there has been contact with a hazardous chemical.	
☐	Know what to do if there is an explosion.	

IDENTIFYING HAZARDS

Visual 2.11

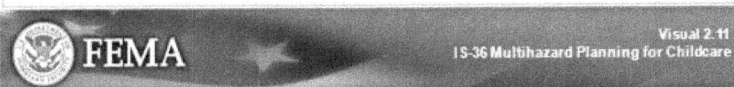

Hazards: Utility Outages

- Know how to use emergency shutoffs for water, gas, and electricity—and mark the shutoffs clearly.
- Have surge protectors.
- Have a land-line phone that does not require electricity.
- Consider purchasing an emergency generator.

FEMA

Visual 2.11
IS-36 Multihazard Planning for Childcare

Key Points

Utility outages and blackouts can occur anywhere, to anyone, at anytime. For prolonged utility outages of more than 2 hours, the main concerns—beyond the safety of children and staff—are minimizing food loss and maximizing comfort.

To prepare for utility outages and blackouts:

- Know how to use emergency shutoffs for water, gas, and electricity—and mark the shutoffs clearly.
- Have surge protectors.
- Have a land-line phone that does not require electricity.
- Consider purchasing an emergency generator, especially if your building is located in an area where power losses are frequent.

Use the job aid on the following page to assess the risk level of a utility outage at your childcare site, and to identify steps you can take to minimize your risk and prepare your site.

Job Aid: Hazard Identification: Utility Outages

Identify Hazard/Threat Risk Level (circle one): *None, Low, Moderate, or High*		
✓	**Steps to reduce my risk:**	**Comments**
☐	Know how to use emergency shutoffs for water, gas, and electricity—and mark the shutoffs clearly.	
☐	Turn off and unplug all unnecessary electrical equipment.	
☐	Have surge protectors.	
☐	Prepare frozen water containers.	
☐	Know how to keep food safe and how to identify if food is safe.	
☐	Have a land-line phone that does not require electricity.	
☐	Consider purchasing an emergency generator, especially if your building is located in an area where power losses are frequent.	

IDENTIFYING HAZARDS

Visual 2.12

Hazards: Crime

- Conduct background or reference checks.
- Ensure doors and windows lock.
- Be familiar with people who should be and should not be around your facility.
- Build a relationship with local law enforcement.
- Have a process for reporting suspicious activity.

FEMA

Visual 2.12
IS-36 Multihazard Planning for Childcare

Key Points

Crime is a problem in every environment. To keep the children in your care safe, follow general crime prevention rules.

- Conduct background/reference checks on all staff to ensure people working at your site have not been arrested or convicted for crimes involving children.
- Ensure doors and windows lock.
- Be familiar with people who should be and should not be around your facility.
- Build a relationship with local law enforcement in your area. Contact police about criminal activity, areas of concern, and prevention recommendations.
- Have a process for reporting anything out of the ordinary.

Use the job aid on the following page to assess the risk level of criminal activity at your childcare site, and to identify steps you can take to minimize your risk and prepare your site.

Job Aid: Hazard Identification: Criminal Activity

Identify Hazard/Threat Risk Level (circle one): None, Low, Moderate, or High		
✓	**Steps to reduce my risk:**	**Comments**
☐	Take precautions to ensure people working at your site have not been arrested or convicted for crimes involving children.	
☐	Ensure doors and windows lock.	
☐	Be aware of people around your facility.	
☐	Build a relationship with local law enforcement in your area.	
☐	Contact police about criminal activity, areas of concern, and prevention recommendations.	
☐	Have a process for reporting anything out of the ordinary.	

IDENTIFYING HAZARDS

Visual 2.13

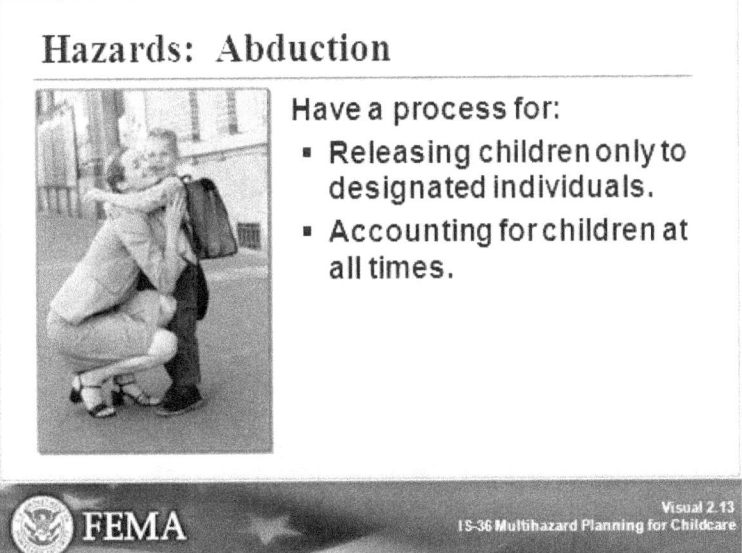

Key Points

"As a parent, I cannot imagine anything more difficult than not knowing where your children are or how they are being treated. Every day across America, children are abducted by family members and acquaintances, and sometimes by strangers. Families traumatized by abduction are faced with the simultaneous challenge of quickly marshaling all available resources to recover their missing child while dealing with the devastation of their loss."

– Assistant Attorney General Laurie O. Robinson

Most children are taken by someone they know. It is essential that childcare centers have a process for:

- Releasing children only to designated individuals.
- Accounting for children at all times.

Use the job aid on the following page to assess the risk level of children being abducted from your childcare site, and to identify steps you can take to minimize your risk and prepare your site.

Job Aid: Hazard Identification: Child Abduction

Identify Hazard/Threat Risk Level (circle one):	*None, Low, Moderate, or High*	
✓	**Steps to reduce my risk:**	**Comments**
☐	Have a process for releasing children including documenting who they can be released to and ensuring any legal orders against a parent or guardian are documented and easily identified before releasing children.	
☐	Have a sign-in/sign-out process that also identifies who can be in areas with children.	
☐	Conduct background/reference checks on all staff.	
☐	Designate how children will be accounted for when in and out of the facility—on field trips, at the playground, during drills.	
☐	Do not share information about a child with anyone but parents or guardians.	
☐	Establish a notification process if a child is missing.	

IDENTIFYING HAZARDS

Visual 2.14

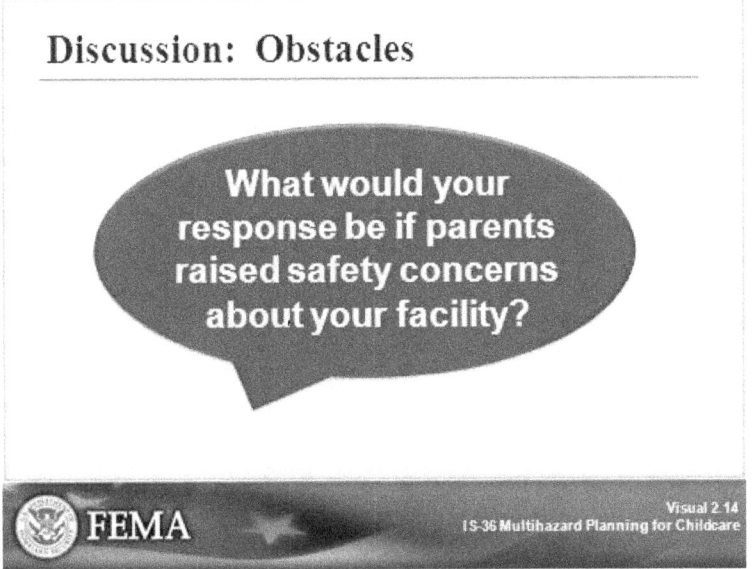

Key Points

What would your response be if parents raised safety concerns about your facility, such as:

- How will you safely get my child out if there is a fire?

- Where do you keep medicines and cleaning products?

- How will you ensure my child cannot get in unsafe areas?

- How will you keep my child safe from electrical hazards?

- To whom will you release my child?

IDENTIFYING HAZARDS

Visual 2.15

Hazards: Severe Weather

- Listen to the radio and NOAA Weather Radio.
- Follow instructions from local officials.
- Stay inside.

FEMA

Visual 2.15
IS-36 Multihazard Planning for Childcare

Key Points

Severe weather can happen anywhere and at any time. It is important to know the types of severe weather risks in your area in order to be prepared.

You can do some simple things to keep the children at your site safe and your property protected when severe weather strikes. When there is a threat of severe weather:

- Listen to the radio and NOAA Weather Radio (a radio with a special receiver to receive information from the network of radio stations that broadcast continuous weather information from the National Weather Service).
- Follow instructions from local officials.
- Stay inside, postpone outdoor activities, and bring children and staff indoors.

It is also important to have a process for closing your facility and to know the meaning of weather terms such as watch, warning, and advisory.

- **Watch:** A watch is used when the risk of a hazardous weather event has increased significantly, but its occurrence, location, and/or timing is still uncertain. It is intended to provide enough lead time so that those who need to set their plans in motion can do so.

IDENTIFYING HAZARDS

Visual 2.15, continued

- **Warning:** A warning is issued when a hazardous weather event is occurring, is imminent, or has a very high probability of occurring. A warning is used for conditions posing a threat to life or property.

- **Advisory:** An advisory highlights special weather conditions that are less serious than a warning. They are for events that may cause significant inconvenience, and if caution is not exercised, the conditions could lead to situations that may threaten life and/or property.

IDENTIFYING HAZARDS

Visual 2.16

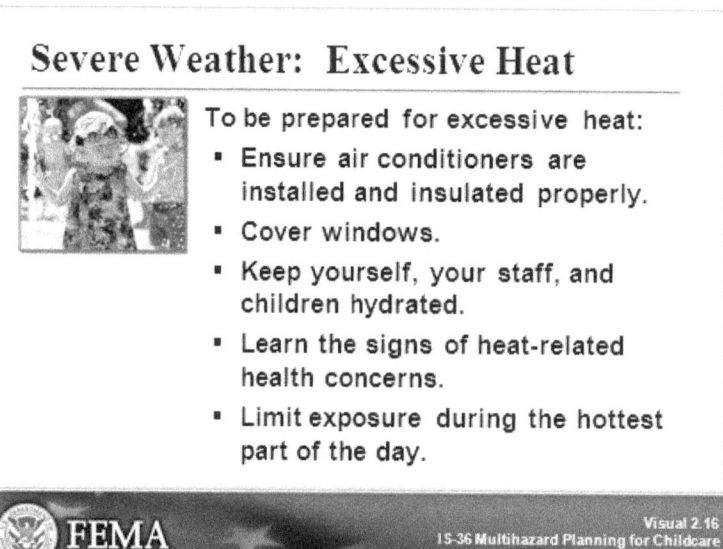

Key Points

In recent years, **excessive heat** has caused more deaths than all other weather-related events. A heat wave is a prolonged period of excessive heat, often combined with humidity. Excessive heat contributes to heat disorders, like heat exhaustion and heat stroke. Older adults and young children are more likely to be impacted by excessive heat. Excessive heat can happen anywhere, but people in urban areas may be at greater risk for prolonged heat waves.

To be prepared for excessive heat in your area:

- Ensure air conditioners are installed and insulated properly.
- Cover windows with drapes, shades, or awnings, or install temporary window reflectors.
- Keep yourself, your staff, and children hydrated.
- Learn the signs of heat-related health concerns.
- Plan activities that limit exposure during the hottest part of the day.

IDENTIFYING HAZARDS

Visual 2.17

Severe Weather: Hurricanes

To be prepared for hurricanes:
- Know the hurricane categories.
- Secure outside items.
- Cover windows.
- Remove damaged limbs from trees.
- Turn off propane tanks and utilities as instructed.
- Ensure you have a supply of water for sanitary purposes.
- Evacuate when instructed.

FEMA

Visual 2.17
IS-36 Multihazard Planning for Childcare

Key Points

Hurricanes and tropical storms have high sustained winds and can produce torrential rains. Hurricane-associated floods, landslides, and mudslides along with high winds cause damage to coastlines and several hundred miles inland. All of the Atlantic and Gulf of Mexico coastal areas and parts of the Southwest and Pacific Coast are subject to the impact of hurricanes and tropical storms. The Atlantic hurricane season lasts from June to November, with the peak season from mid-August to late October.

To be prepared for hurricanes and tropical storms:

- Know the differences between the hurricane categories.
- Secure outside items or bring them inside.
- Cover windows with pre-cut plywood or shutters.
- Remove damaged/diseased limbs from trees.
- Turn off propane tanks.
- Turn off utilities as instructed; otherwise, turn refrigerators to highest setting.
- Ensure you have a supply of water for sanitary purposes; fill bathtub and other large containers.
- Evacuate when instructed by local officials.

IDENTIFYING HAZARDS

Visual 2.18

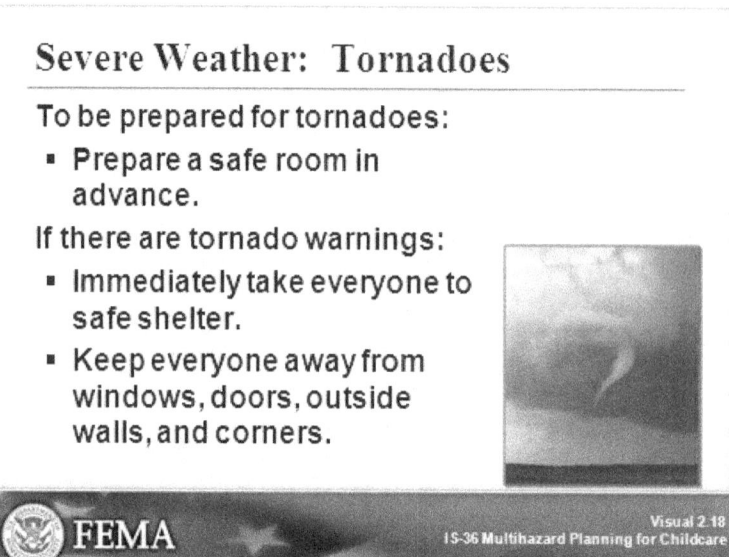

Key Points

Tornadoes are the most violent of storms with winds that usually exceed 100 mph and can devastate a neighborhood in seconds. A thunderstorm is the first step in the development of a tornado; if conditions are right, then a tornado may develop. Tornadoes can appear without warning and can be transparent until dust and debris are picked up. Tornadoes have been reported in every State and can occur at any time of the year. Danger signs of tornadoes are dark or greenish skies; large hail; large, dark, low-lying clouds; and a loud roar, similar to a freight train.

To be prepared for tornadoes:

- Prepare a safe room in advance: storm cellar or basement, interior room or hallway on lowest floor possible.

If there are tornado warnings:

- Immediately take everyone to safe shelter.
- Keep everyone away from windows, doors, outside walls, and corners.

IDENTIFYING HAZARDS

Visual 2.19

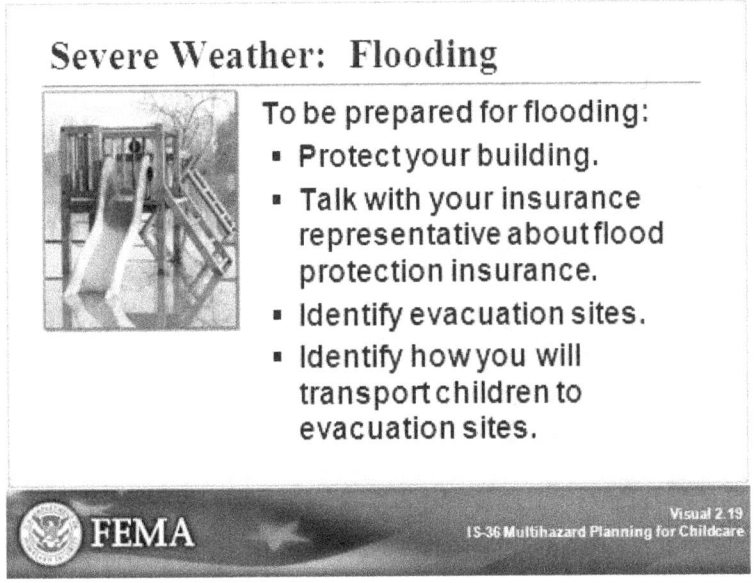

Key Points

Flooding is the most common disaster in the United States. Floods develop differently and can be caused by extended periods of heavy rain, tropical storms and hurricanes, warming after a heavy snow, or flash floods. Every State is at risk of flood hazards. Be especially aware if you live in low-lying areas near water or downstream from a dam. Know your risk of flooding and flash flooding and be familiar with the terms that identify floods: flood watch, flash flood watch, flood warning, and flash flood warning.

To be prepared for floods:

- Protect your building: elevate furnace, water heater, and electrical panel; seal basements with waterproofing; install "check valves."
- Talk with your insurance representative about flood protection insurance.
- Identify evacuation places that are on higher ground.
- Identify how you will transport children to evacuation sites.

In the event of a flood:

- Keep informed about whether water is safe to drink.
- If you have to evacuate, secure your site and turn off utilities, if instructed.
- Avoid floodwaters and moving water.
- Keep children out of the water.
- Stay away from downed power lines.

IDENTIFYING HAZARDS

Visual 2.20

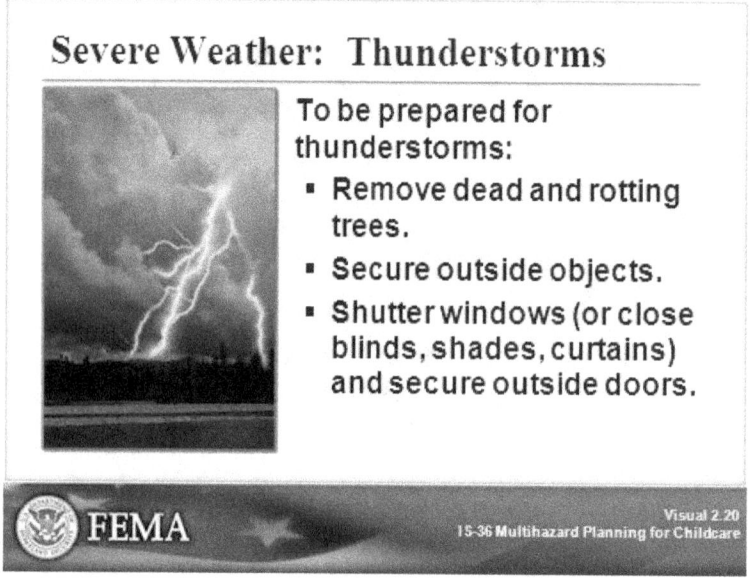

Key Points

Every **thunderstorm** produces lightning and, on average, lightning kills 300 people and injures 80 people per year in the United States. Lightning is unpredictable; it can strike as far as 10 miles from any rainfall. Other thunderstorm-related dangers are tornadoes, strong winds, hail, wildfire, and flash flooding.

To be prepared for thunderstorms:

- Remove dead and rotting trees.
- Secure outside objects.
- Shutter windows (or close blinds, shades, curtains) and secure outside doors.

If thunderstorms are forecasted, limit or cancel outdoor activities.

During a thunderstorm:

- Take everyone indoors.
- Do not take baths or showers, or use plumbing or electrical appliances.

Note: Lightning can occur without rain. According to the National Oceanic and Atmospheric Administration (NOAA) National Severe Storms Laboratory, dry lightning is cloud-to-ground lightning without any rain nearby. This kind of lightning is more likely to cause forest fires.

IDENTIFYING HAZARDS

Visual 2.21

Severe Weather: Winter Storms

To be prepared for winter storms:

- Have rock salt, sand, and snow shovels on hand.
- Ensure you have extra blankets and adequate clothing for children.
- Make sure your site is well insulated.
- Insulate pipes and allow faucets to drip a little during cold weather.
- Know how to shut off water valves.
- Be careful when using alternate heat sources.
- Have a supply of extra food and water.

FEMA

Visual 2.21
IS-36 Multihazard Planning for Childcare

Key Points

The National Weather Service calls **winter storms** "deceptive killers" because of the number of deaths indirectly related to the storms, including traffic accidents, fire, and hypothermia. Even areas that normally experience mild winters can experience major winter storms and extreme cold. Primary concerns with winter storms are the potential loss of heat, power, and telephone, and a shortage of supplies.

To be prepared for winter storms:

- Have rock salt, sand, and snow shovels on hand.
- Ensure you have extra blankets and adequate clothing for children.
- Make sure your site is well insulated.
- Insulate pipes and allow faucets to drip a little during cold weather.
- Know how to shut off water valves.
- Be careful when using alternate heat sources. The U.S. Fire Administration has issued tips on fire safety during and after a winter storm.
- Have a supply of extra food and water.

Use the job aid on the following page to assess the risk level from severe weather, and to identify steps you can take to minimize your risk and prepare your site.

Job Aid: Hazard Identification: Severe Weather

Identify Hazard/Threat Risk Level (circle one): *None, Low, Moderate, or High*	
✓ **Steps to reduce my risk:**	**Comments**
Severe Weather – General ☐ Have a NOAA Weather Radio on site. ☐ When there is a threat of severe weather, listen to the radio or television and a NOAA Weather Radio for information. ☐ Listen to instructions from local officials. ☐ If severe weather has been forecasted, stay inside, postpone outdoor activities, and bring children and staff indoors. ☐ Have a process for closing the facility and notifying parents/guardians and staff. ☐ Know weather terms—watch, warning, advisory.	
Excessive Heat ☐ Ensure air conditioners are installed and insulated properly. ☐ Install temporary window reflectors. ☐ Cover windows with drapes, shades, or awnings. ☐ Keep yourself, staff, and children hydrated. ☐ Be aware of signs of heat-related health concerns.	
Hurricanes/Tropical Storms ☐ Know the differences between the hurricane categories. ☐ Secure outside items or bring them inside. ☐ Cover windows with pre-cut plywood or shutters. ☐ Remove damaged/diseased limbs from trees. ☐ Turn off utilities as instructed; otherwise, turn refrigerators to their highest setting. ☐ Turn off propane tanks. ☐ Ensure you have a supply of water for sanitary purposes; fill bathtub and other large containers. ☐ Evacuate when instructed by local officials.	
Tornadoes ☐ Prepare a safe room in advance: storm cellar or basement, interior room or hallway on lowest floor possible. ☐ If you are under a tornado warning, immediately take everyone to safe shelter. ☐ Keep everyone away from windows, doors, outside walls, and corners.	

Job Aid: Hazard Identification: Severe Weather (Continued)

Identify Hazard/Threat Risk Level (circle one): None, Low, Moderate, or High	
✓ **Steps to reduce my risk:**	**Comments**
Flooding ☐ Protect your building: elevate the furnace, water heater, and electrical panel; seal the basement with waterproofing; and install "check valves." ☐ Talk with your insurance representative about flood protection insurance. ☐ Have plans to move to higher ground. ☐ Keep informed about whether water is safe to drink. ☐ If you have to evacuate, then secure your site and turn off utilities, if instructed. ☐ Avoid floodwaters and moving water. Keep children out of water. ☐ Stay away from downed power lines.	
Thunderstorms ☐ Remove dead and rotting trees. ☐ Secure outside objects. ☐ Shutter windows (or close blinds, shades, curtains) and secure outside doors. ☐ If you can hear thunder, go indoors. ☐ During a thunderstorm, do not take baths or showers or use plumbing or electrical appliances.	
Winter Storms and Extreme Cold ☐ Have rock salt, sand, and snow shovels. ☐ Ensure you have extra blankets and adequate clothing for children. ☐ Make sure your site is well insulated. ☐ Insulate pipes and allow faucets to drip a little during cold weather. ☐ Know how to shut off water valves. ☐ Be careful when using alternate heat sources. ☐ Have a supply of extra food and water.	

IDENTIFYING HAZARDS

Visual 2.22

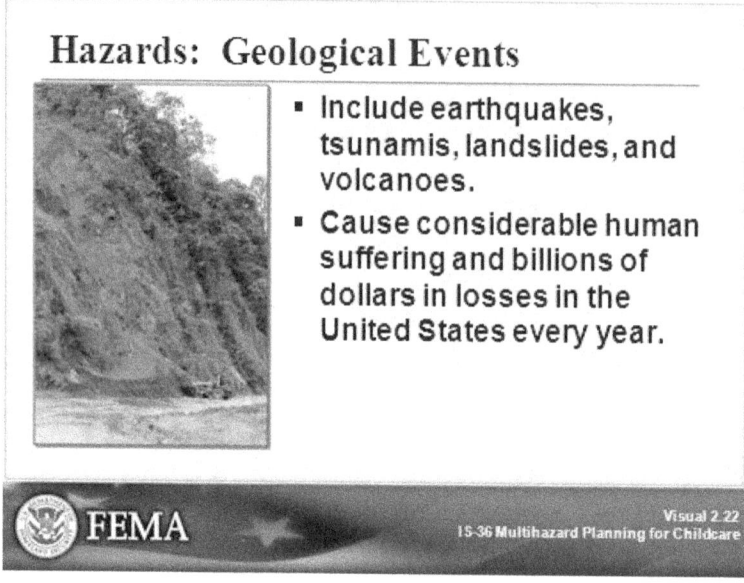

Key Points

You may be in an area where geological events are also a concern. According to the U.S. Geological Survey, geologic hazards, such as earthquakes, landslides, volcanic eruptions, coastal erosion, and floods, result in considerable human suffering and billions of dollars in losses in the United States every year.

IDENTIFYING HAZARDS

Visual 2.23

Geological Events: Earthquakes

To be prepared for an earthquake:

- Familiarize yourself with earthquake terms.
- Fasten/secure heavy items.
- Place sleeping and sitting areas away from hazards (pictures, mirrors, lamps, etc.).
- Mark and clear exits.
- Know how to shut off gas valves.
- Have an emergency kit ready.

FEMA

Visual 2.23
IS-36 Multihazard Planning for Childcare

Key Points

An **earthquake** is one of the most frightening and destructive incidents that can happen. An earthquake is the sudden movement of the earth caused by the breaking and shifting of rock beneath the earth's surface. One can occur without notice any time of the day and year. Every region of the United States is at risk of earthquakes, with 45 States and territories at moderate to high risk.

To be prepared for an earthquake:

- Familiarize yourself with earthquake terms.
- Fasten/secure heavy items and furniture to wall studs and brace overhead light fixtures.
- Place cribs, sleeping mats, and sitting areas away from hazards that can fall in or on them (pictures, mirrors, lamps, etc.).
- Clear exits and ensure there are at least two exits for evacuation. Make sure all exits are clearly marked.
- Know how to shut off gas valves.
- Have an emergency kit ready.

When shaking starts:

- Drop, cover, and hold.
- Keep everyone away from windows.
- Stay inside until the shaking stops. (Be prepared for aftershocks.) Research has shown that most injuries occur when people inside buildings attempt to move to a different location inside the building or try to leave.

IDENTIFYING HAZARDS

Visual 2.24

Geological Events: Tsunamis

If there is the possibility of a tsunami:
- Listen to local officials.
- Be prepared to act quickly and evacuate.
- Stay away from low-lying coastal areas.

FEMA

Visual 2.24
IS-36 Multihazard Planning for Childcare

Key Points

Tsunamis are enormous waves caused by underwater disturbances such as earthquakes. The waves created travel in all directions, and waves that approach the shore build in height. The first waves can reach the shore before any warning has been issued. A tsunami can strike anywhere along the U.S. coastline, but the most destructive have been along the California, Washington, Alaska, and Hawaii coasts. A dramatic recession of water is nature's warning of a tsunami. Hazards from tsunamis include drowning, flooding, contamination of drinking water, and fires.

If there is the possibility of a tsunami:

- Listen to local officials.
- Be prepared to act quickly and evacuate inland.
- Stay away from low-lying coastal areas if a tsunami warning has been issued.

IDENTIFYING HAZARDS

Visual 2.25

Key Points

Landslides can be caused by natural incidents (earthquakes, storms, fires, or volcanoes) or human modification of land. In a landslide, masses of rock, earth, or debris move either slowly or rapidly, destroying property and possibly taking lives. Landslides occur in all States and territories of the United States.

To be prepared for landslides and debris flows:

- Be familiar with whether debris flows have occurred in your area.
- Watch how water flows during storms.
- If in imminent danger, evacuate your site immediately

IDENTIFYING HAZARDS

Visual 2.26

Hazards: Volcanoes

If there is the possibility of a volcanic eruption:
- Listen to local officials.
- Bring children inside.
- Shut windows and doors to maintain air quality.
- Be prepared to evacuate quickly.
- Include goggles and nose and mouth protection in your emergency supply kits.

FEMA
Visual 2.26
IS-36 Multihazard Planning for Childcare

Key Points

A **volcano** is a vent in the earth that, when pressure builds and it erupts, releases dangerous molten rock and gases. Volcanoes are mainly a concern for Hawaii, Alaska, and the Pacific Northwest.

If there is the possibility of a volcanic eruption:

- Listen to local officials.
- Bring children inside.
- Shut windows and doors to maintain air quality.
- Be prepared to evacuate quickly.
- Include goggles and nose and mouth protection in your emergency supply kits.

Use the job aid on the following page to assess the risk level of geological events and to identify steps you can take to minimize your risk and prepare your site.

Job Aid: Hazard Identification: Geological Events

Identify Hazard/Threat Risk Level (circle one): None, Low, Moderate, or High	
✓ **Steps to reduce my risk:**	**Comments**
<u>Earthquakes</u> ☐ Familiarize yourself with earthquake terms. ☐ Fasten/secure heavy items and furniture to wall studs and brace overhead light fixtures. ☐ Place cribs, sleeping mats, and sitting areas away from hazards that can fall in or on them (pictures, mirrors, lamps, etc.). ☐ Clear exits and ensure there are at least two exits for evacuation. Make sure all exits are clearly marked. ☐ Know how to shut off gas valves. ☐ Have an emergency kit ready. ☐ When shaking starts, drop, cover, and hold; keep everyone away from windows; and stay inside until the shaking stops. (Be prepared for aftershocks.)	
<u>Tsunamis</u> ☐ Listen to local officials. ☐ Be prepared to act quickly and evacuate inland.	
<u>Landslides and Debris Flows</u> ☐ Follow proper land-use procedures. ☐ Be familiar with whether debris flows have occurred in your area. ☐ Watch how water flows during storms. ☐ If in imminent danger, evacuate your site immediately.	
<u>Volcanoes</u> ☐ Listen to local officials. ☐ Bring children inside. ☐ Shut windows and doors to maintain air quality. ☐ Be prepared to evacuate quickly. ☐ Include goggles and nose and mouth protection in your emergency supply kits.	

IDENTIFYING HAZARDS

Visual 2.27

Hazards: Illness and Food Safety

- Know:
    - Which illnesses require the child to be excluded.
    - How parents will be notified.
    - How regular health checks will be conducted.
- Take steps to prevent food-borne illness.

FEMA

Visual 2.27
IS-36 Multihazard Planning for Childcare

Key Points

Two other hazards you may need to prepare for are:

- **Illness Outbreaks:** When children get sick, it is important that your site is prepared to manage the illness by knowing:
    - Which illnesses require the child to be excluded.
    - How parents will be notified of illnesses that arise at the childcare site.
    - How regular health checks will be conducted.

- **Food Safety:** Because childcare providers are often in the role of serving children food, it is important that you also take steps to prevent food-borne illness and are careful about what you serve children in your care.

Use the job aid on the following page to assess the risk level of an illness outbreak and of food safety hazards or threats at your childcare site, and to identify steps you can take to minimize your risk and prepare your site.

Job Aid: Hazard Identification: Illness Outbreaks and Food Safety

Identify Hazard/Threat Risk Level (circle one):	*None, Low, Moderate, or High*	
✓ **Steps to reduce my risk:**		**Comments**
<u>Illness Outbreaks</u> ☐ Avoid close contact with people who are sick. Advise staff to stay home when they are sick and ask parents to keep sick children home. ☐ Cover your mouth and nose with a tissue when coughing or sneezing. ☐ Clean your hands often. ☐ Avoid touching your eyes, nose, and mouth. ☐ Practice good health habits: get plenty of sleep, be physically active, manage your stress, drink plenty of fluids, get your flu shot, and eat nutritious foods. ☐ Require proper immunization of children in your care. ☐ Have disinfectant/cleaning processes for bathrooms (including changing tables and children's potties), food preparation areas (including dishes, high chairs, and utensils), toys, beds, and bedding. ☐ Establish a policy for handling sick children: exclusion, dismissal, and care. ☐ Clean/sanitize hands between handling of children.		
<u>Food Safety</u> ☐ If you prepare food at your site, follow food safety procedures: clean, separate, cook, and chill. ☐ Know how to properly store foods – including breast milk, formula, and baby food. ☐ Know foods not to serve due to child choking hazards. ☐ Ensure everyone knows of any children's food allergies, and how to respond if a child has an allergic reaction. ☐ Know when to save and when to throw out food after power outages.		

MITIGATING HAZARDS

Visual 2.28

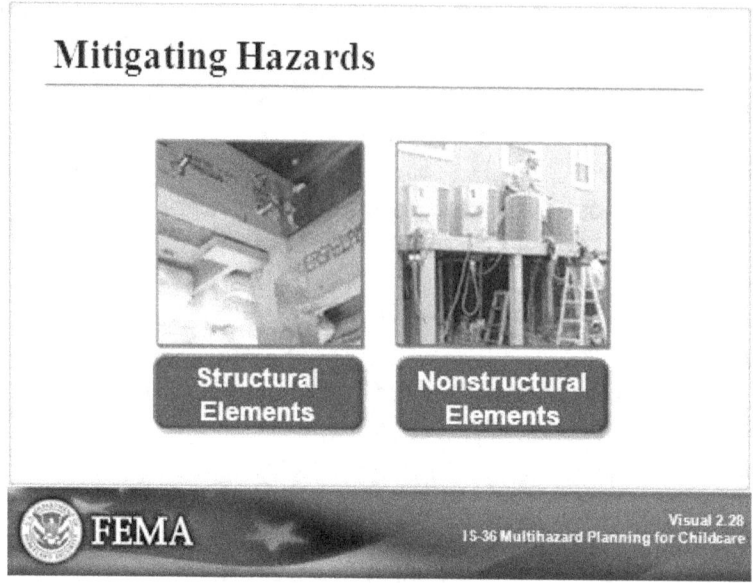

Key Points

Now that you have considered the hazards and threats facing your childcare site, you also need to consider how to mitigate (lessen) hazards specific to the structural and nonstructural elements of your facility's building and grounds.

- **Structural elements** include any component of the building whose primary function is to support the dead load (e.g., building, roof).

- **Nonstructural elements** include any portion of the building or grounds not connected to the main structure (e.g., bookshelves, file cabinets, furnishings).

Use the job aid on the following page to identify items in the building or surrounding grounds that may pose a hazard.

Job Aid: Building and Grounds Mitigation Checklist

Area:	
Surveyed by:	
Date Surveyed:	
✓ **Hazard**	**Mitigation Measures**
Building ☐ Extended, unsupported roof spans ☐ Large windows or panes of glass, especially if: • Not composed of safety glass • Located near exits or evacuation routes ☐ Suspended ceilings and light fixtures ☐ Incompatible chemicals stored in close proximity or not stored in a manner to withstand falling and breaking ☐ Hazardous materials located in areas that do not have warning signs ☐ Paper or other combustibles (e.g., greasy rags) stored near heat source ☐ Unsecured heavy or unstable items, including: • Portable room dividers • Appliances (e.g., water heaters, space heaters, microwave ovens) • Filing cabinets, bookcases, and wall shelves • Athletic equipment • Vending machines • TV monitors • Wall-mounted objects • Aquariums • Table lamps • Hanging plants above seating areas ☐ Electrical equipment	
Grounds ☐ Equipment in need of repair ☐ Rocks or other material that could cause injury ☐ Fences in need of repair ☐ Exposed nails, screws, or bolts ☐ Trees or shrubs that present a fire hazard or wind hazard or provide areas for an intruder to hide ☐ Streams in close proximity ☐ Electrical wires ☐ Gasoline or propane tanks ☐ Natural gas lines	

MITIGATING HAZARDS

Visual 2.29

Next Steps

- Identify hazards and threats.
- Develop strategies to address hazards and threats.
- Identify members from the community to assist.
- Develop and implement a process to identify and address new hazards.

FEMA
Visual 2.29
IS-36 Multihazard Planning for Childcare

Key Points

Your next steps are to:

- Identify hazards and threats that are of the highest consequence and most likely for your site.
- Develop strategies to address those hazards and threats. (Use the hazard and mitigation worksheets provided earlier in this module for guidance.)
- Identify members from the community to review and comment on your strategies and identify hazards or threats that are missing. Include community members such as:
  - Local/county emergency manager.
  - Parents.
  - First responders.
  - Local schools/school district.
  - State department of health.
  - Childcare site insurance carrier.
  - Utility company personnel.
  - Local business and industry personnel.
  - Childcare organizations.
- Develop and implement a process to regularly check for new hazards and address them as needed.

MITIGATING HAZARDS

Visual 2.30

Activity

Instructions: Working individually...

1. Identify three hazards that may affect your childcare facility.
2. Identify three actions you can take to reduce the risk of each hazard.
3. Be prepared to share your results in 15 minutes.

FEMA

Visual 2.30
IS-36 Multihazard Planning for Childcare

Key Points

Purpose: This activity will give you the opportunity to identify hazards in your childcare facility.

Instructions: Working individually . . .

1. Identify three hazards that may affect your childcare facility.
2. Identify three actions that you can take to reduce the risk of each hazard.
3. Be prepared to share your results in 10 minutes.

HAZARDS	ACTIONS
1.	1. 2. 3.
2.	1. 2. 3.
3.	1. 2. 3.

MODULE SUMMARY

Visual 2.31

Module Summary

Can you now:

- Identify hazards and threats that impact your childcare site?
- Describe how to prevent or mitigate the impact of likely and high-consequence hazards and threats?

FEMA
Visual 2.31
IS-36 Multihazard Planning for Childcare

Key Points

This module provided information on identifying and preparing for hazards.

Below are some additional resources that can help you address hazards.

- The Federal Emergency Management Agency (FEMA) has information on including the whole community to help you prepare to address hazards: www.fema.gov
- The National Association of Child Care Resource & Referral Agencies (NACCRRA) has information for childcare sites: www.naccrra.org
- The U.S. Fire Administration site has a smoke alarm safety quiz you can take: www.usfa.dhs.gov
- Ready.gov and the American Red Cross provide information on additional types of hazards and threats and how to address them:
  - www.ready.gov
  - www.redcross.org
- The Floodsmart.gov Web site provides additional information on flooding and flood risks: www.floodsmart.gov
- The Food and Drug Administration, the U.S. Department of Agriculture, and Foodsafety.gov have information on food safety:
  - www.fda.gov
  - www.fsis.usda.gov
  - www.foodsafety.gov
- Flu.gov provides updated information on the flu: www.flu.gov
- FEMA's Multihazard Emergency Planning for Schools toolkit has tools and resources that can be useful for emergency planning: training.fema.gov/emiweb/emischool

MODULE 3: DEVELOPING PLANS

MODULE INTRODUCTION

Visual 3.1

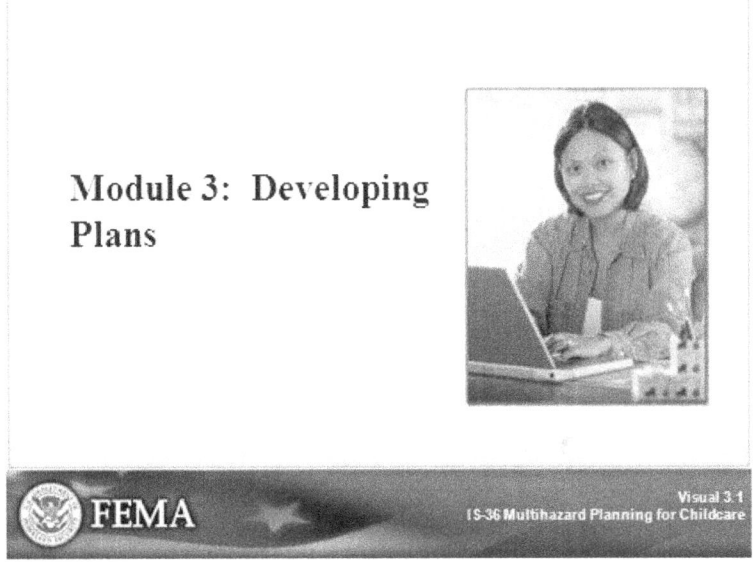

Key Points

This lesson introduces you to the second step in being prepared: developing plans. During this step, you will take the hazards and threats that you determined to be of high consequence and most likely and identify what you will do when something happens. Developing processes and procedures to put in place will help you respond effectively in emergency situations.

MODULE INTRODUCTION

Visual 3.2

Module Objectives

- Describe procedures to follow when an emergency occurs.
- Identify how your childcare site will recover from an emergency.
- Describe how to develop and maintain your emergency plan.

FEMA

Visual 3.2
IS-36 Multihazard Planning for Childcare

Key Points

By the end of this module, you should be able to:

- Describe procedures to follow when an emergency occurs.
- Identify how your childcare site will recover from an emergency.
- Describe how to develop and maintain your emergency plan.

EMERGENCY PLANS

Visual 3.3

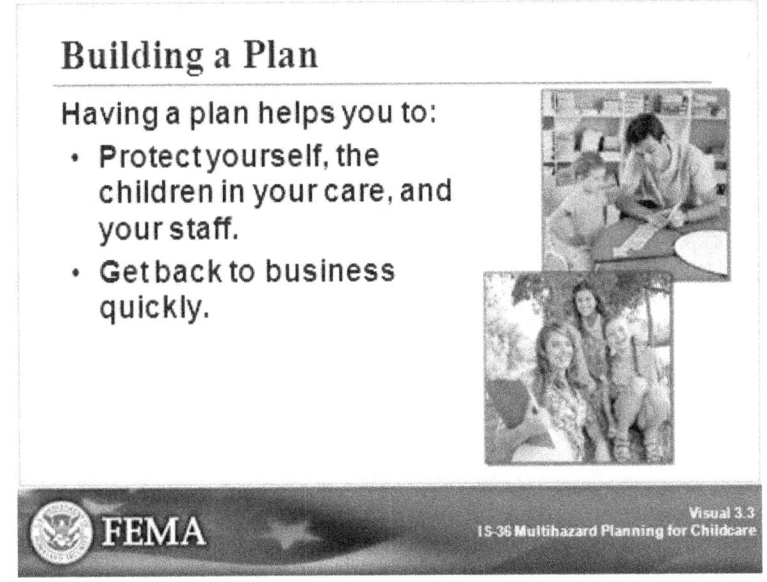

Key Points

You are responsible for protecting yourself, the children in your care, and your staff, and for getting back to business quickly. To meet these responsibilities, you need a plan.

First, it is critical in an emergency that you are able to contact parents and emergency services. Your plan should include ways to collect, maintain, and easily access contact information. Depending on what happens, you may have to evacuate your site, or stay put to keep everyone safe. To prepare for an evacuation, identify evacuation routes and exits, where you will go, what you will take with you, and how you will account for children.

If sheltering, identify safe locations in your site, supplies to have, and if necessary, how to seal a room. Whether you stay or go, you will need emergency supplies. Do you have an adequate amount of water, food, flashlights, batteries, radios, medicine, and first aid supplies? Regularly check to make sure everything works and nothing has expired.

A comprehensive plan needs to address the different needs of the children and staff to ensure everyone is protected. And no matter the size of your site, someone is relying on your services. If an emergency impacts your site, your plan needs to include ways to recover quickly.

To put together an effective, comprehensive plan, include people from your community at all stages in the process. Members of your community bring skills and expertise. Get input from emergency management officials, first responders, parents, local businesses, and organizations.

Finally, update your plan regularly. A plan that sits on the shelf is not effective.

Emergencies happen. You need to have a plan—to be ready.

EMERGENCY PLANS

Visual 3.4

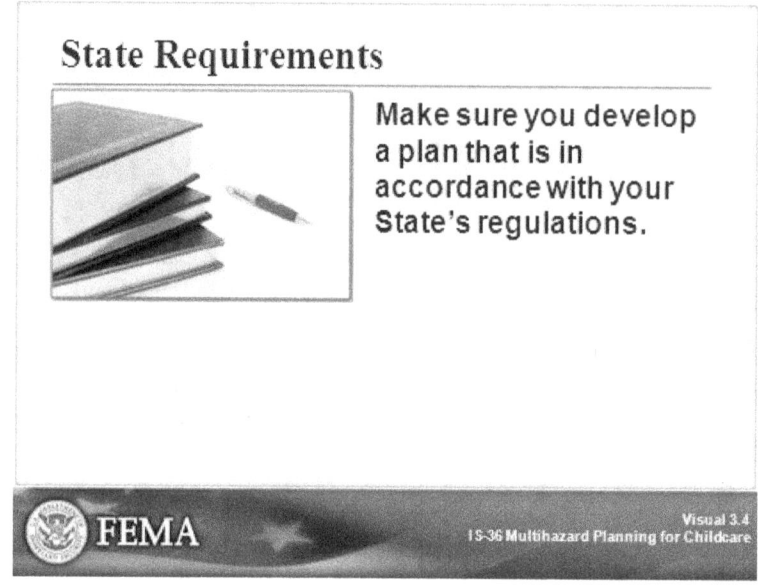

Key Points

Many States require that childcare sites have an emergency plan and specify what it must include. Make sure you are familiar with these requirements in order to develop a plan that is in accordance with your State's regulations.

The U.S. Department of Health and Human Services, Administration for Children & Families Web site has a listing of State requirements: http://www.acf.hhs.gov

EMERGENCY PLANS

Visual 3.5

Planning and Preparedness Issues

- Child contact information
- Emergency contact information
- Documented procedures
- Emergency supplies

FEMA

Visual 3.5
IS-36 Multihazard Planning for Childcare

Key Points

You need to focus on the following areas for emergency planning and preparedness:

- **Child contact information** including:
  - Parent/guardian contact information.
  - Emergency contact information (not parent or guardian).
  - Medical conditions and allergies.
  - Pediatrician contact information.
  - Child's personal preferences.
  - Permission for medical transport and treatment.

- **Emergency contact information** posted in obvious locations that lists:
  - Fire, emergency, and police.
  - Water, utility, and gas companies.

- **Documented procedures** for:
  - Tracking entry and exit of children and visitors.
  - Site closure.
  - Sheltering-in-place.
  - Evacuation.
  - Meeting care/support requirements during emergencies for children with access and functional needs.

EMERGENCY PLANS

Visual 3.5, continued

- **Emergency supplies**, including:
  - Food, water, and basic emergency supplies.
  - First aid.
  - Supplies specific to the children at your site (diapers, formula, games, toys, personal care and hygiene).
  - NOAA Weather Radio.

EMERGENCY PLANS

Visual 3.6

Activity

Instructions: Working individually...

1. Review the list of planning and preparedness issues in your Student Manual.

2. Determine if you have a process to address each issue at your childcare site.

3. List any issues that you may need to address.

FEMA

Visual 3.6
IS-36 Multihazard Planning for Childcare

Key Points

Purpose: This activity will give you the opportunity to identify planning and preparedness issues that need to be addressed at your childcare site.

Instructions: Working individually . . .

1. Review the list of planning and preparedness issues in your Student Manual, located on the previous pages.
2. Determine if you have a process to address each issue at your childcare site.
3. List any issues that you may need to address.

CONTACT INFORMATION

Visual 3.7

Child Contact Information

- Parent/guardian contact information
- Designated people with permission to pick up child
- Designated physician and hospital
- Child's favorite toys, foods, and things to do
- Comforting techniques for the child
- Description from health provider of special health care needs

FEMA — Visual 3.7 / IS-36 Multihazard Planning for Childcare

Key Points

Make sure your plan includes all the information you need to quickly contact parents or guardians. If you have not been collecting information on parents or if you need to collect additional information, provide them with a form to obtain the information you need.

At a minimum, request:
- Parent/guardian contact information:
  - Phone numbers: home, work, and cell.
  - Email: home and work.
  - Work: Supervisor contact information, address.
  - At least two emergency contacts—one local and one long distance.
- Designated people with permission to pick up child, other than parent/guardian.
- Designated physician and hospital.
- Child's favorite toys, foods, and things to do.
- Comforting techniques for the child.
- Description from health provider of special health care needs including allergies, medications, and dietary concerns.

You need to have processes in place to collect and regularly update contact information for children:
- When they initially sign up at your site.
- When information changes.
- At predetermined intervals—for example, at the beginning of your community's school year.

The job aid on the following pages includes a sample Child Information Sheet.

Job Aid: Child Information Sheet

Child's Information:	Date:

First Name: _____ Last Name: _____

Address: _____

Allergies/Special Instructions/Comforting Techniques/Favorite Foods, Toys, Things To Do:

_____

_____

_____

Parent/Guardian Information (1):

First Name: _____ Last Name: _____

Relationship to Child: _____

Address (if different
from child): _____

Home Phone: _____ Cell Phone: _____

Home Email: _____

Work Phone: _____

Work Email: _____

Work Name and
Address: _____

Supervisor Name: _____ Supervisor Phone: _____

Parent/Guardian Information (2):

First Name: _____ Last Name: _____

Relationship to Child: _____

Address (if different
from child): _____

Home Phone: _____ Cell Phone: _____

Home Email: _____

Work Phone: _____

Work Email: _____

Work Name and
Address: _____

Supervisor Name: _____ Supervisor Phone: _____

Job Aid: Child Information Sheet, continued

Emergency Contact Information (1):	
First Name: _____	Last Name: _____
Relationship to Child: _____	
Address: _____	
Home Phone: _____	Cell Phone: _____
Work Phone: _____	

Emergency Contact Information (2):	
First Name: _____	Last Name: _____
Relationship to Child: _____	
Address: _____	
Home Phone: _____	Cell Phone: _____
Work Phone: _____	

Emergency Contact Information (3):	
First Name: _____	Last Name: _____
Relationship to Child: _____	
Address: _____	
Home Phone: _____	Cell Phone: _____
Work Phone: _____	

Doctor Information:	
Pediatrician Name: _____	
Pediatrician Address: _____	
Pediatrician Phone: _____	
Additional Medical Information:	

Other:
Other instructions, concerns, restrictions:

CONTACT INFORMATION

Visual 3.8

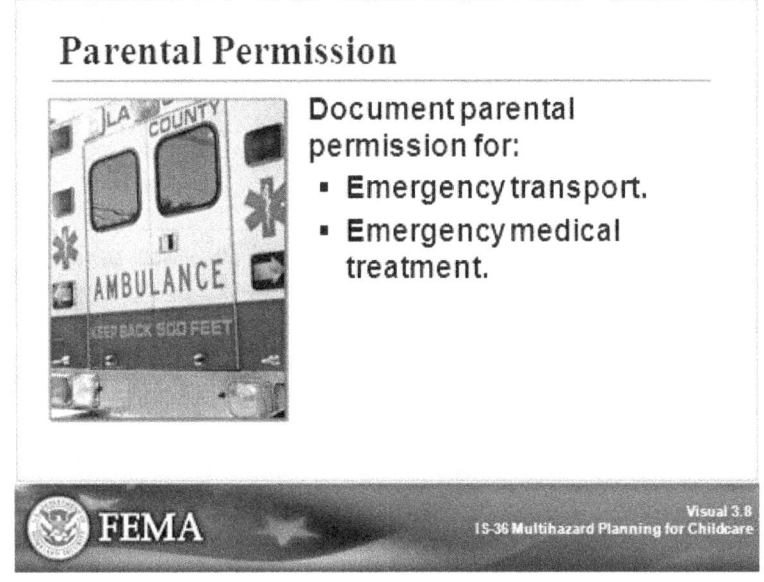

Key Points

It is important to document parental permission for emergency transport and emergency medical treatment. In an emergency, it may not always be possible to send a child to his/her primary care provider.

The job aids on the following page include a sample Emergency Transport Permission Form and Emergency Treatment Permission Form.

Job Aid: Emergency Transport Permission Form

This form authorizes emergency transportation for a child. This form does not authorize or guarantee treatment.

I, _____ **give/do not give** permission to _____
   (parent or guardian name)   *(circle appropriate choice)*   *(name of childcare provider)*

to transport my child, _____ to _____
                    (child's name)   *(hospital name)*

or the nearest emergency location for emergency medical care.

**Parent/Guardian
Signature:** _____ **Date:** _____

Job Aid: Emergency Treatment Permission Form

This form authorizes emergency treatment for a child.

I, _____ **give/do not give** permission to _____
   (parent or guardian name)   *(circle appropriate choice)*   *(name of childcare provider)*

to have my child, _____ treated by a licensed medical professional.
                (child's name)

**Parent/Guardian
Signature:** _____ **Date:** _____

CONTACT INFORMATION

Visual 3.9

Emergency Contact Information

- Medical personnel and hospital
- Police, fire, and rescue
- Poison control
- Local emergency management
- Utility companies
- Emergency information sources
- Insurance
- Neighbors

FEMA   Visual 3.9
IS-36 Multihazard Planning for Childcare

Key Points

In addition to knowing how to contact parents or guardians, you need to be able to quickly contact emergency personnel when something happens.

Post emergency contact information in obvious locations and include names, phone numbers, and email addresses for the following resources:

- Medical personnel and hospital
- Police, fire, and rescue
- Poison control
- Local emergency management
- Utility companies
- Emergency information sources (radio stations, TV stations, NOAA radio frequency for your area)
- Insurance
- Neighbors

The job aid on the following page includes a sample emergency contact sheet.

Job Aid: Sample Emergency Contact Sheet

Post this sheet in obvious locations in case of an emergency.	Name	Phone	Email
Medical Emergency (911)			
Police (911)			
Fire (911)			
Rescue (911)			
Hospital			
Poison Control (800-222-1222)			
Local Emergency Management			
Electric Company			
Gas Company			
Water Company			
Waste Disposal			
Insurance Provider			

Emergency Information Sources

Local Television Stations	Channel: _____ Phone: _____ Contact: _____ Channel: _____ Phone: _____ Contact: _____ Channel: _____ Phone: _____ Contact: _____ Channel: _____ Phone: _____ Contact: _____
Local Radio Stations	Station: _____ Phone: _____ Contact: _____ Station: _____ Phone: _____ Contact: _____ Station: _____ Phone: _____ Contact: _____ Station: _____ Phone: _____ Contact: _____
NOAA Weather Station	Frequency: _____ *For your area frequency, go to: http://www.nws.noaa.gov/nwr/listcov.htm*

PROCEDURES

Visual 3.10

Procedures: Sign-In and Sign-Out

Enable you to:

- Know who is at your site and who is not.
- Easily account for children during an emergency.

FEMA

Visual 3.10
IS-36 Multihazard Planning for Childcare

Key Points

An important component of planning and preparedness is having documented procedures to address emergency situations.

Another simple but important process to ensure the safety and security of your children and site is implementing sign-in and sign-out procedures. These procedures are necessary so you know who is at your site and who is not, especially during an emergency. You need to be able to easily account for children during an emergency. You do not want to spend valuable time looking for a child who has left or did not show up that day.

If you have a large population of children at your site, you may need to implement attendance procedures for each group of children. In such circumstances, ensure your staff knows which children they have the responsibility to track.

If you have many visitors that stay on site, you may need to include them in your sign-in/sign-out procedures.

The job aid on the following page includes a sample sign-in/sign-out sheet. As children are dropped off and picked up, have the authorized parent or guardian sign the child in or out.

Job Aid: Sign-In/Sign-Out Sheet

Child's Name	Time In	Time Out	Parent/Guardian	Staff Releasing

PROCEDURES

Visual 3.11

Procedures: Closing

Include:

- Who will make the decision to close the site.
- How the decision will be made.
- How you will notify parents or guardians.
- When parents, guardians, and staff will be notified of site closing.

FEMA

Visual 3.11
IS-36 Multihazard Planning for Childcare

Key Points

You may need to close your site because of weather, utility outages, emergency situations, or extreme illness.

In case of a site closure, effective procedures for notifying parents or guardians are essential. Identify:

- Who will make the decision to close the site.
- How the decision will be made (for example, weather, road conditions, local school district closings, etc.).
- How you will notify parents or guardians.
- When parents, guardians, and staff will be notified of site closing.

Use the job aid on the following page to identify roles, responsibilities, and processes for when you need to close your childcare site.

Job Aid: Site Closing Procedures

Specify how each of the following procedures will be implemented.
The decision to close the facility will be made by: • • •
The decision will be based on (weather forecasts, school closings, road reports, etc.):
Time by which the decision to close will be made (night before, early morning before first child arrives):
Parents will be notified of the closing by: •   Text message to parents/guardians. •   Television (identify station(s)):   •   Radio (identify station(s)):   •   Phone calls to each parent (telephone trees are helpful if your facility serves many families): Who will call? How will you note the call was made? What is the process if you cannot contact a parent?
The following message will be placed on the facility phone line with closing information:
List additional procedures for your site below:

PROCEDURES

Visual 3.12

Key Points

In some emergency situations, it may be best to stay in your site to remain safe—for example, when a tornado has been spotted or if local officials tell you the air outside is unsafe or if there is a police chase in your neighborhood. This is known as "sheltering-in-place."

Start by identifying where you will take everyone for:

- Weather concerns (e.g., tornado). Select a room in the basement or an interior room on the lowest level away from corners, windows, doors, and outside walls.
- Contaminated air. If local authorities say that air is badly contaminated and recommend sheltering, you will need to shelter in a room where you can create a barrier between you and the contaminated air.
- Outside dangers (e.g., threats from criminals or dangers from wild animals). If there is a threat outside, you will need to bring and keep everyone inside to keep them safe. This practice or procedure is often called a reverse evacuation.

PROCEDURES

Visual 3.13

Procedures: Sheltering-in-Place

- If outside, have children and staff go inside.
- Notify everyone of the need to shelter.
- Account for all children and staff.
- Have everyone go to the identified shelter location.
- Ensure you have emergency supplies in the shelter location.
- Listen to the radio for instructions.

FEMA

Visual 3.13
IS-36 Multihazard Planning for Childcare

Key Points

Determine procedures to follow for sheltering-in-place, including:

- If outside, have children and staff go inside as quickly as possible.
- Notify everyone of the need to shelter.
- Account for all children and staff.
- Have everyone go to the identified shelter location.
- Ensure you have emergency kits, first aid kits, phones, and radios in the shelter location.
- Listen to the radio for instructions.

Use the job aid on the following page to identify roles, responsibilities, and processes for sheltering-in-place at your childcare site.

Job Aid: Shelter-in-Place Procedures

Specify how each of the following procedures will be implemented.
Identify shelter locations (Who will identify? How will they be identified? Will there be multiple locations?):
Ensure shelter locations: • Are clearly marked. • Are free of items that may fall during sheltering. • Have emergency lighting and sufficient ventilation.
The decision to shelter-in-place will be made by:
The decision to shelter will be based on (notification from local officials, weather forecasts, etc.):
911 will be called by:
Staff will be notified of sheltering and where to shelter by (announcement, phone call, etc.):
Staff will account for the children under their care, including: • Bringing children inside. • Taking attendance at appropriate points in the process (designate). • Getting children to designated sheltering rooms.
Designated staff will bring to the shelter location(s): • Emergency kits. • First aid kits. • Supplies for sealing rooms, if necessary. • Activities for children.
Designated staff who will monitor the radio for instructions:
For contaminated air scenarios, designated staff will: • Seal the room. • Close curtains or blinds. • Shut off HVAC systems.
List additional procedures for your site below:

PROCEDURES

Visual 3.14

Procedures: Contaminated Air

- Shut and lock doors and windows.
- Turn off air conditioner, heat, and/or fans.
- Seal the room by taping up windows, vents, and exhausts.
- Close curtains or blinds.
- If air starts to bother children or staff, hold wet cloths over the nose and mouth or go into the bathroom, close the door, and turn on the shower.

FEMA

Visual 3.14
IS-36 Multihazard Planning for Childcare

Key Points

If you are notified to shelter because of contaminated air, you will need to take some additional precautions:

- Shut and lock all outside doors, windows, and as many internal doors as possible.
- Turn off air conditioner, heat, and/or fans.
- Seal the room by taping up windows, vents, and exhausts—any opening to the outside—with plastic wrap, aluminum foil, or wax paper and duct tape.
- Close curtains or blinds.
- If air starts to bother children or staff, hold wet cloths over the nose and mouth or go into the bathroom, close the door, and turn on the shower.

PROCEDURES

Visual 3.15

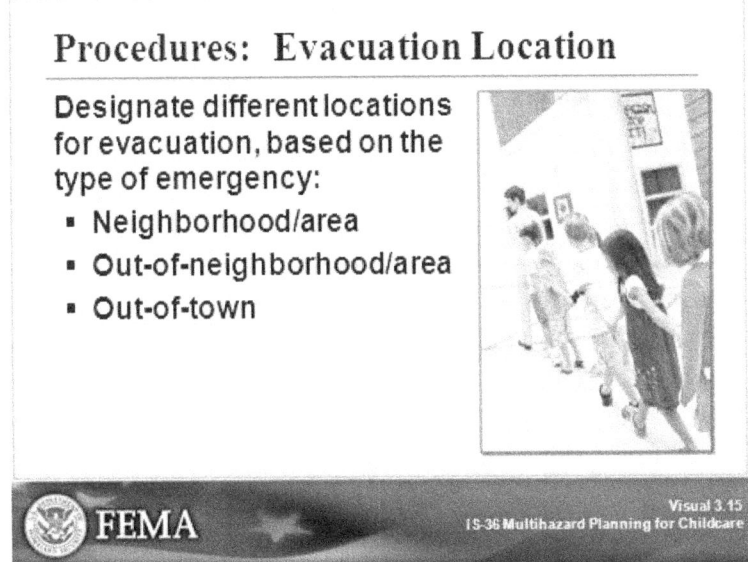

Key Points

In some emergency situations—fire, explosion, and some weather and geological events—it will not be safe to stay in or around your facility.

You should designate three different locations for evacuation, based on the type of emergency:

- **Neighborhood/area evacuation site.** This location is someplace close to your facility and will be used when you need to evacuate but your neighborhood is still safe (for example, there's a fire at your facility).

- **Out-of-neighborhood/area evacuation site.** This site is further away from your facility and would be used for a more widespread threat (for example, wildfire, gas leak, or flooding).

- **Out-of-town evacuation site.** This site would be a place to go when your town or city is inaccessible or being evacuated (for example, in the event of an environmental hazard, widespread flooding, or a hurricane).

PROCEDURES

Visual 3.16

Procedures: Evacuation

Determine:

- When an evacuation is necessary.
- Who will call 911.
- What evacuation routes and sites will be used.
- How you will get children out.
- Who will take emergency kits.
- When and how you will account for children.
- How children will be transported to evacuation sites.
- Any special considerations.

FEMA

Visual 3.16
IS-36 Multihazard Planning for Childcare

Key Points

Your evacuation procedures should address:

- Who determines when an evacuation is necessary?
- Who will call 911?
- What evacuation routes, sites, and exits should be used?
- How will you get children out (e.g., using a buddy system; identifying people to assist; using cribs, wagons, and strollers to enable one person to evacuate several children; etc.)?
- Who will take emergency kits?
- When and how will you account for children?
- How will children be transported to long-distance evacuation sites?
- Any special considerations.

Use the job aid on the following page to identify roles, responsibilities, and processes for evacuation at your childcare site.

Job Aid: Evacuation Procedures

Specify how each of the following procedures will be implemented.	
Evacuation routes and exits will be designated and posted by:	
Evacuation site locations will be communicated to parents by:	
Evacuation sites are: • Neighborhood: • Out-of-neighborhood: • Out-of-town:	We will get to the sites by: • Walking • Using staff or facility vehicles • Using staff or facility vehicles
Evacuation specifics for: • Infants (e.g., use evacuation cribs or have infant carrying devices) • Children with access and functional needs	
The decision to evacuate will be made by:	
The decision to evacuate will be based on:	
911 will be called by:	
Staff will be notified of evacuation and where to evacuate to by (announcement, phone call, etc.):	
Emergency kits and medications will be brought to the evacuation site by:	
Utilities will be shut off by:	
Facility will be secured by:	
Staff will account for the children in their care: • Prior to evacuation by: • At an initial safe location by: • At the evacuation site by:	
Parents will be notified of the evacuation by: • Person responsible: • Process for notification (phone, email, local media notification):	
List additional procedures for your site below:	

PROCEDURES

Visual 3.17

Procedures: Reunification

- Reunification locations
- Parent notification of your designated evacuation sites
- Requirements for release of children
- Procedures for:
  - Documenting that the child was picked up
  - Children that are missing or not present that day
  - Children not picked up

FEMA

Visual 3.17
IS-36 Multihazard Planning for Childcare

Key Points

If you have to evacuate your site and cannot return to it, you need to know how you will reunite children with their parents or guardians.

Your reunification procedures should address:

- Reunification locations.
- Parent notification of your designated evacuation sites.
- Requirements for release of children (showing identification, filling out child release forms, being listed among those who can pick child up, etc.).
- Process for documenting that the child was picked up.
- Procedures if child is missing or was not present that day.
- Procedures for children not picked up (e.g., identifying other contacts (grandparents, relatives), notifying authorities).

Reunification procedures are closely linked to your other procedures. If you have clearly defined evacuation procedures, clear sign-in and sign-out processes, and updated contact information, you will more likely have a seamless reunification process.

Use the job aid on the following page to identify roles, responsibilities, and processes for reuniting children with parents/guardians if you have to evacuate your childcare site.

Job Aid: Reunification Procedures

Specify how each of the following procedures will be implemented.
Notify parents/guardians of evacuation sites (identify who will tell parents/guardians, how will they be notified, etc.): • In advance of evacuation: • When evacuating: • After evacuating:
Children can be picked up by: • Parents/guardians designated on emergency contact sheets.   • Others identified on emergency contact sheets.
Designated staff will account for the children under their care and have a record of who was picked up by whom by (identify the staff, process, documents, etc.):
Special procedures for when a child is transported for medical care (identify who will accompany children, where they will go, how you will account for them, etc.):

PROCEDURES

Visual 3.18

Procedures: Additional Assistance

Your plan must address how you will support:

- Infants and toddlers.
- Children with additional needs such as medication or equipment.

Visual 3.18
IS-36 Multihazard Planning for Childcare

FEMA

Key Points

Children, especially young children (infants and toddlers), often require additional assistance in an emergency. It is important that your preparedness planning addresses how you will support each child in your care.

Your plan also needs to address those children in your care with other additional needs such as medication, equipment (service animals, wheelchairs, glasses, crutches, etc.), and communication requirements.

During your planning, think about what children with access and functional needs might need if there were:

- No water or electricity.
- No access to medication.
- Separation from family.
- Lack of health care or emergency services.
- No access to formula, baby food, or other dietary items.

Use the job aid on the following page to identify roles, responsibilities, and processes to ensure the needs of all children are included in your emergency plan.

Job Aid: Children With Access and Functional Needs

Specify how each of the following procedures will be implemented.

Track any access and functional requirements and how they will be addressed:
• Create a list of children with access and functional needs and identify if the needs are temporary.
• Identify accommodations for:
   o Normal operations.
   o Sheltering.
   o Evacuation.
   o Drills and practice.
   o No water or electricity.
• Include information on medications, equipment, and allergies.
• Assign staff to the children with access and functional needs.
• Identify, provide, and track any training required to care for the child.

Identify processes for medications and other equipment during an emergency: • Included in emergency kit. • How to transport. • How to store.
How you will ensure medical personnel are aware of child's needs: • Forms you will provide. • Who will get copies of forms? Emergency transport? Doctors? Other caregivers?
Special procedures to follow when child is transported for medical care (identify who will accompany the child, any accommodations required during transport, etc.):

EMERGENCY SUPPLIES

Visual 3.19

Emergency Supplies

For sheltering:
- Enough food, water, and other items to last for 72 hours for each child and adult

For evacuating:
- Supplies in something easy to carry

FEMA

Visual 3.19
IS-36 Multihazard Planning for Childcare

Key Points

You will need an emergency kit when sheltering and evacuating.

These kits should include:

- **For sheltering:** Enough food, water, and other items to last for 72 hours for each child and adult.

- **For evacuating:** Supplies in something easy to carry (e.g., backpacks or roller bags).

Use the job aids on the following pages to identify items you need for your emergency kits for sheltering and for evacuation.

Job Aid: Emergency Kit Checklist for Sheltering

✓	Item
	Emergency contact information for children and staff
	Disposable diapers
	Water (1 gallon per person per day – 3 gallons per person)
	Food (do not include any items that any of the children have allergies to)
	Battery-powered or hand-crank radio and a NOAA Weather Radio with tone alert and extra batteries for both
	Flashlight and batteries (in each room)
	Non-electric can opener
	Medications
	Disposable cups, bowls, plates, utensils
	Paper towels, toilet paper
	Hand sanitizer
	Blankets
	Whistle to signal for help
	Dust mask
	Moist towelettes, garbage bags, and plastic ties for personal sanitation
	Wrench or pliers to turn off utilities
	Cell phone with charger, inverter, or solar charger
	Clothing for each person (jacket, pants, shirt, shoes, hat, gloves)
	Blanket or sleeping bag for each person
	Rain gear
	Fire extinguisher
	Matches in waterproof container
	Signal flare
	Paper and pencil
	Household chlorine bleach (keep in a secure location, away from children's access)

Job Aid: Emergency Kit Checklist for Evacuation

✓	Item
	Emergency contact information for children and staff
	First aid kit
	Medications
	Dry or canned infant formula
	Water
	Granola/energy bars (remember to take into consideration children's food allergies when packing the emergency kits)
	Books, games, toys
	Safety blankets
	Cell phone and charger
	Money (cash or traveler's checks)
	Compass
	Matches in waterproof container

RECOVERY

Visual 3.20

Recovery (1 of 2)

- Identify where you will conduct operations if you are not able to use your site.
- List needed supplies and sources.
- Identify companies and resources for restoring your site.
- Take photographs of the interior and exterior of your site.
- Maintain a current inventory of equipment and supplies for insurance.

FEMA

Visual 3.20
IS-36 Multihazard Planning for Childcare

Key Points

After an emergency, you will want to return to operations as quickly as possible. Careful planning can help make recovery more efficient. You need to consider how you will restore your physical site, business operations, and the physical and emotional well-being of both children and staff after a disaster.

To get up and running quickly after an incident, you need to plan for how you will restore your physical site in both the short term and the long term.

- Identify where you will conduct both short-term and long-term operations if you are not able to use your site.
- List the supplies you will need to operate and where you will get them.
- Identify companies and resources for restoring your site (e.g., debris removal, repairs, painting, construction, and/or landscaping).
- Take photographs of the interior and exterior of your site and store them in a safe place. These photographs can be used for insurance claims.
- Maintain a current inventory of equipment and supplies for insurance.

RECOVERY

Visual 3.21

Recovery (2 of 2)

Identify:

- Where you will store your business records.
- How you will let parents and guardians know your site is closed and when it will reopen.
- Contracts or agreements to put in place for alternate sites and services.

FEMA
Visual 3.21
IS-36 Multihazard Planning for Childcare

Key Points

In order to return to operating your business as soon as possible, in your planning process identify:

- Where you will store your business records.
  - ○ Store important documents in a waterproof, fireproof container.
  - ○ Consider having duplicate records offsite in case those at your site are destroyed.
  - ○ Have a backup plan for electronic files.

- How you will let parents and guardians know your site is closed and when it will reopen.
  - ○ Have up-to-date contact information in your records.
  - ○ Provide parents with emergency contact information for you and your childcare center.

- Contracts or agreements to put in place for alternate sites and services.

RECOVERY

Visual 3.22

Psychological and Emotional Recovery

- Observe children's behavior and accept the changes.
- Listen to children's concerns and feelings.
- Keep normal routines.
- Be calm and reassuring.
- Limit media exposure.
- Teach calming techniques.
- Provide support to the child's family.

FEMA

Visual 3.22
IS-36 Multihazard Planning for Childcare

Key Points

After an incident, people may experience both psychological and emotional impacts. It is important to plan for how you will address children's needs, including the following considerations:

- Observe children's behavior and accept the changes.
- Listen to children's concerns and feelings.
- Keep normal routines.
- Be calm and reassuring.
- Limit media exposure.
- Teach calming techniques.
- Provide support to the child's family.

Find out if your local community or schools have psychological recovery information and tools available for your site.

The job aid on the following page lists tips for managing the psychological impacts of an incident.

Job Aid: Tips for Managing the Psychological Impacts of an Incident

Childcare providers have a role in managing psychological trauma following an incident, including:

- **Identify at-risk children.**
  Victims that have been physically or sexually abused may be at a higher risk of developing post-traumatic stress.

- **Develop partnerships with local mental health practitioners.**
  Immediately after an incident, there are often enough caregivers to assist victims with short-term grief. Over time, the availability of resources for long-term treatment dwindles. Reaching out to social workers, psychologists, and other mental health practitioners in the community helps you secure access to these long-term services.

- **Strengthen and encourage peer support.**
  Victims can draw strength and develop coping strategies from friends in their peer group. Additionally, these friendships help decrease isolation and encourage discussion.

- **Look for symptoms of psychological stress, including:**
  - **Preschool:** Thumb sucking, bedwetting, clinging to parents, sleep disturbances, loss of appetite, fear of the dark, regression in behavior, and/or withdrawal from friends and routines.
  - **Elementary/middle school:** Irritability, aggressiveness, clinginess, nightmares, school avoidance, poor concentration, and/or withdrawal from activities and friends.
  - **High school:** Sleeping and eating disturbances, agitation, increase in conflicts, physical complaints, delinquent behavior, and/or poor concentration.

- **Support recovery by designing activities that:**
  - **Encourage students to talk about disaster-related events.**
    Children need an opportunity to discuss their experiences in a safe, accepting environment. Although group discussions are a good vehicle for validating children's feelings about their experiences, it is important to end such discussion on a positive note by focusing on things that promote a sense of security, mastery, or preparedness. This positive wrap-up may come from students themselves, and teachers can reinforce or elaborate on these points.
  - **Promote positive coping and problem-solving skills.**
    Activities should teach children how to apply problem-solving skills to incident-related stressors. Children should be encouraged to develop realistic and positive methods of coping that increase their ability to manage their anxiety, and to identify which strategies fit with each situation.
  - **Encourage friendship and peer support among students.**
    Children with strong emotional support from others are better able to cope with adversity. Relationships with peers can provide suggestions for how to cope with difficulties and can help decrease isolation.

Job Aid: Tips for Managing the Psychological Impacts of an Incident, continued

Example Activities:

- **Preschool and Elementary School Activities:**
  - Encourage class activities in which children can organize or build projects (scrapbooks, replicas, toys, etc.) to give them a chance to organize and process what may be chaotic and confusing feelings and events.
  - Encourage games and physical activity to relieve tension and anxiety.
  - Ask children to draw pictures of the incident or whatever comes to their minds. Talking about the picture later with a teacher or in a small group may help them to process their experiences and discover that others share their fears, sadness, etc.
  - Have children either write or listen to short stories about the incident. This activity can help children verbalize fears as well as get back in touch with previous positive associations about a disruption.
  - Children can draw, write, or talk about what they remember, or respond to questions or topics such as:
    - What happened after the storm hit?
    - How did you help your family during or after the disaster?
    - How could you help your family if you were in another disaster?
    - Did anything good or positive happen because of the disaster? Did you learn anything from what happened to you?

- **Middle School/Junior High and High School Activities:**
  Childcare providers can use many of the basic principles outlined in the suggestions for younger children with older students. In addition:
  - Give children opportunities to use art, music, or poetry to describe experiences and express feelings.
  - Encourage children to keep a journal, or write and produce a play or a video.

RECOVERY

Visual 3.23

Support to Parents and Staff

Describe:

- Steps to take to assist others in regaining a positive attitude and reducing stress.
- Recovery resources that are available in the community.

FEMA

Visual 3.23
IS-36 Multihazard Planning for Childcare

Key Points

Your plan also needs to address how you will support parents and staff after an incident.

This part of your plan might describe:

- Steps to take to assist others in regaining a positive attitude and reducing stress (e.g., encourage exercise, identify support groups, and encourage making time for family and friends).
- Recovery resources that are available in the community (e.g., shelters, childcare resource and referral agency).

PUTTING YOUR PLAN TOGETHER

Visual 3.24

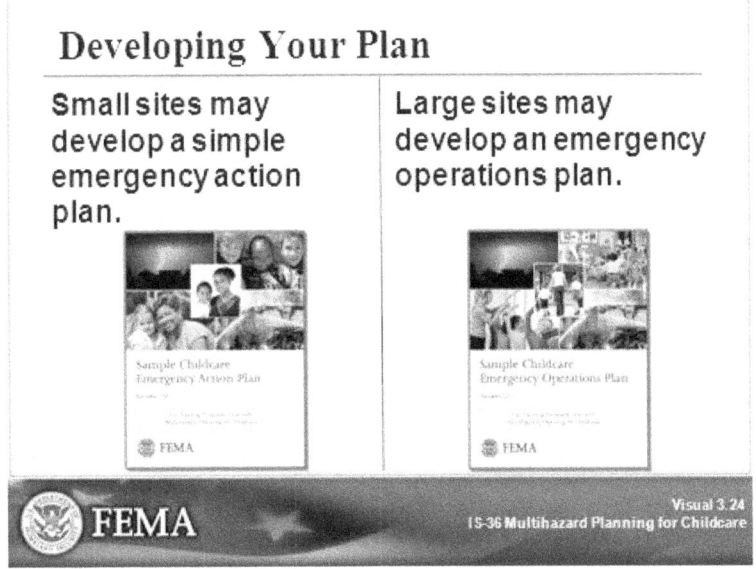

Key Points

Now that you understand the procedures you need to develop to be prepared, let's look at how to put these together in a plan. The type of plan you choose for your site is based on the number of children cared for and the complexity of your site.

Small sites may develop a simple emergency action plan that includes:

- How to contact parents/guardians.
- What medical information you need to collect on each child.
- How to contact emergency services.
- What to do if you need to stay put (shelter-in-place).
- What to do if you need to leave your site (evacuate).
- How to get children back to their parents/guardians (reunification).
- How you will accommodate the needs of each child in your care.

PUTTING YOUR PLAN TOGETHER

Visual 3.24, continued

Large sites may develop an emergency operations plan (EOP) that includes:

- **A basic plan:** Describes expected hazards, outlines roles and responsibilities, and explains how you keep the plan current.
  - Introductory Material
  - Purpose, Scope, Situation Overview, and Assumptions
  - Concept of Operations
  - Organization and Assignment of Responsibilities
  - Direction, Control, and Coordination
  - Communications
  - Administration, Finance, and Logistics
  - Plan Development and Maintenance
  - Authorities and References

- **Functional annexes:** Describe procedures and missions for many hazards. Examples include: evacuation, shelter-in-place, and parent-child reunification.

- **Hazard-specific annexes:** Describe strategies for managing specific hazards.

What type of plan do you have or might you use?

PUTTING YOUR PLAN TOGETHER

Visual 3.25

Who Reviews Your Plan?

- Local/county emergency manager
- Parents
- First responders
- Local schools and local school district
- State department of health
- Childcare site insurance carrier
- Utility company personnel
- Local business and industry personnel
- Childcare organizations

FEMA

Visual 3.25
IS-36 Multihazard Planning for Childcare

Key Points

Once you have a plan, it needs to be reviewed; whether it is a simple emergency action plan or a more formal emergency operations plan.

Include those people in your community that you solicited for input into your plan as part of your review and approval process, including:

- Local/county emergency manager.
- Parents.
- First responders.
- Local schools/school district.
- State department of health.
- Childcare site insurance carrier.
- Utility company personnel.
- Local business and industry personnel.
- Childcare organizations.

The Federal Emergency Management Agency (FEMA) encourages engaging the whole community in your planning process.

PUTTING YOUR PLAN TOGETHER

Visual 3.26

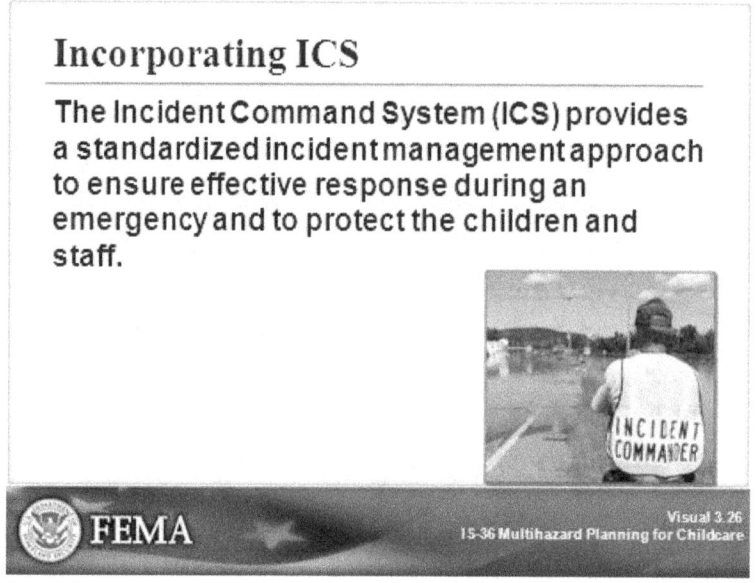

Incorporating ICS

The Incident Command System (ICS) provides a standardized incident management approach to ensure effective response during an emergency and to protect the children and staff.

Visual 3.26
IS-36 Multihazard Planning for Childcare

Key Points

As part of your emergency plan, your site may want to include Incident Command System (ICS) principles. ICS provides a standardized incident management approach to ensure effective response during an emergency and to protect the children and staff.

To become familiar with ICS principles, structure, and roles, FEMA has the following independent study courses available:

- IS-100.SC: Introduction to the Incident Command System for Schools
- IS-700: National Incident Management System (NIMS), An Introduction

PUTTING YOUR PLAN TOGETHER

Visual 3.27

Activity

Instructions: Working individually, answer the following questions:

- What processes and procedures are you missing?
- What do you need to add?
- What processes and procedures do you have in place?
- How can you improve existing processes and procedures?

FEMA

Visual 3.27
IS-36 Multihazard Planning for Childcare

Key Points

Purpose: This activity will give you the opportunity to identify procedures that need to be added or improved in your emergency plan.

Instructions: Working individually, review your plan and answer the following questions:

- What processes and procedures are you missing?

- What do you need to add?

- What processes and procedures do you have in place?

- How can you improve existing processes and procedures?

MODULE SUMMARY

Visual 3.28

Module Summary

Can you now:

- Describe procedures to follow when an emergency occurs?
- Identify how your childcare site will recover from an emergency?
- Describe how to develop and maintain your emergency plan?

FEMA

Visual 3.28
IS-36 Multihazard Planning for Childcare

Key Points

Some resources to assist your childcare site with the development of your plan are listed below:

- The U.S. Department of Health and Human Services, Administration for Children & Families has information on States' requirements about emergency planning for childcare sites: www.acf.hhs.gov
- The U.S. Department of Education has information on crisis planning and recovery for communities and schools: www.ed.gov
- The National Clearinghouse for Educational Facilities has information on emergency planning, preparedness, and response: www.ncef.org
- The U.S. Department of Health and Human Services has an emergency preparedness toolkit with general planning tips and information on evacuation and sheltering: www.hhs.gov
- FEMA's Comprehensive Preparedness Guide (CPG) 101 has information on developing an emergency operations plan: www.fema.gov/about/divisions/cpg.shtm

MODULE 4: TESTING AND UPDATING YOUR PLAN

MODULE INTRODUCTION

Visual 4.1

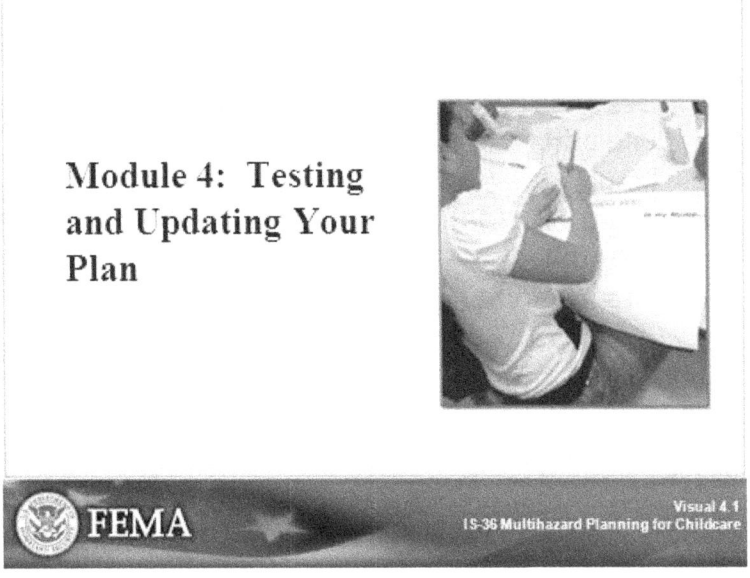

Key Points

This module introduces you to the third step in being prepared: testing and updating your plan. During this step, you communicate, train, and practice the procedures you identified. You then use information from training, exercising, and communicating to update your plan.

MODULE INTRODUCTION

Visual 4.2

Module Objectives

- Describe how you will communicate, train, and practice your preparedness procedures.
- Identify the emergency preparedness information you will share with your community.
- Describe when to update your plan.

FEMA
Visual 4.2
IS-36 Multihazard Planning for Childcare

Key Points

By the end of this module, you should be able to:

- Describe how you will communicate, train, and practice your preparedness procedures.
- Identify the emergency preparedness information you will share with your community.
- Describe when to update your plan.

MODULE INTRODUCTION

Visual 4.3

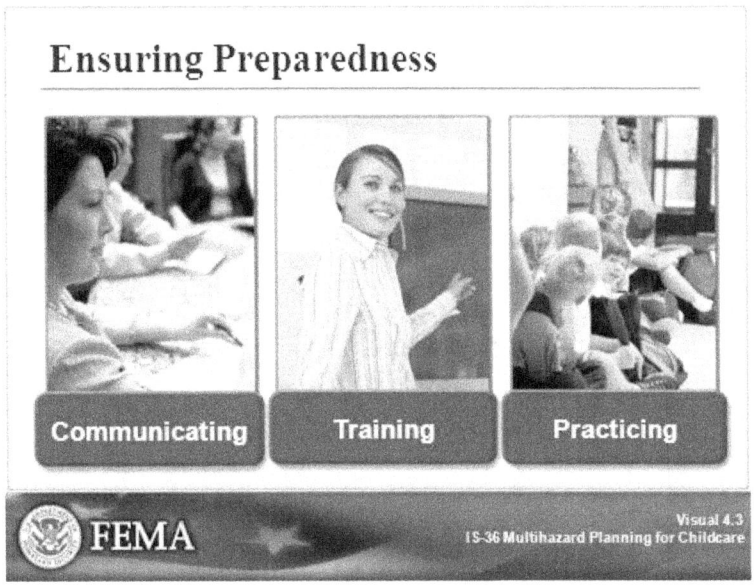

Key Points

Once you have identified procedures to address your hazards, you then need to identify who needs to know the procedures, how you will tell them, and how you will make sure they work.

Everyone who works at your site must be ready to act if something happens. To ensure preparedness:

- **Communicate:** Talk to staff and volunteers about your site's emergency procedures and encourage them to have personal/family emergency plans.

- **Train:** Conduct internal training on your procedures and also consider external training, such as:
    - Community Emergency Response Team (CERT) training (training on disaster preparedness for hazards in your area; check for local availability through your local emergency management office).
    - First aid training.
    - FEMA independent study courses.

- **Practice:** Conduct drills on your procedures, including:
    - Evacuation.
    - Sheltering-in-place.
    - Drop, cover, and hold.
    - Reunification.

COMMUNICATING

Visual 4.4

Communicating: Children

- Give children advance warning about drills and what to expect.
- Stay calm.
- Use activities to make emergency preparedness fun and memorable.
- Make your communication age-appropriate.

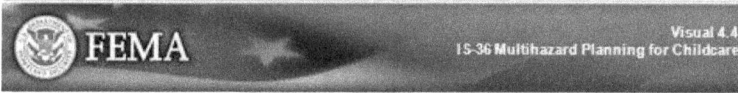

FEMA

Visual 4.4
IS-36 Multihazard Planning for Childcare

Key Points

You want children to be informed and prepared, but you do not want to scare them when you share information about your plan and emergency procedures.

Some things to consider before training and practicing are:

- Give children advance warning about drills and what to expect; also explain what happened at the completion of the drill.
- Stay calm.
- Use games, rhymes, music, art, and other activities to make emergency preparedness fun and memorable.
- Make your communication age-appropriate. For example, for:
  - **Toddlers:** Include toddlers in the drills. Provide them with simple instructions, and use rhymes and games to help them learn.
  - **Preschool children:** Give simple instructions and reassure these youngsters that they and your site are safe.
  - **Elementary and middle school children:** Allow the children to ask questions. Make sure they understand the difference between reality and fantasy.
  - **High school children:** Include high school children in discussions about how to keep the site safe.

COMMUNICATING

Visual 4.5

Communicating: Parents

Provide information on:

- Your evacuation locations.
- How you will shelter when necessary.
- Where you will take any injured children.
- What you need from them for emergency kits.
- How you will notify them of site closure.
- The importance of family preparedness plans.

FEMA

Visual 4.5
IS-36 Multihazard Planning for Childcare

Key Points

It is critical that parents know the details in your plan. Telling them what your procedures are will make them confident in your ability to protect their children. Include information on:

- Your evacuation locations.
- How you will shelter when necessary.
- Where you will take any injured children—doctors, hospitals, clinics.
- What you need from them for emergency kits—clothes, blankets, medicine.
- How you will notify them of site closure.
- The importance of family preparedness plans.

Note: Emergency cards are a good way to get important information to parents.

COMMUNICATING

Visual 4.6

Communicating: First Responders

Include emergency management and first responders so they will:

- Be familiar with your site and plans.
- Know your evacuation locations.
- Know how to best communicate with you and alert you to area emergencies.
- Help you improve your plan and your procedures.
- Provide training.

FEMA

Visual 4.6
IS-36 Multihazard Planning for Childcare

Key Points

Including emergency management and first responders in your training and practice will enable them to:

- Be familiar with your site and plans.
- Know your evacuation locations.
- Know how to best communicate with you and alert you to area emergencies.
- Provide input to help you improve your plan and your procedures.
- Provide training for your staff and children in various emergency response areas of expertise (fire, police, etc.).

TRAINING

Visual 4.7

Key Points

Training can be delivered in different ways to accommodate the schedules and needs of your site.

Some types of training include:

- **Briefings:** Short meetings that provide information about a specific topic (e.g., new evacuation sites, tips on how to contact parents).

- **Seminars/classroom training:** Used to introduce new programs, policies, or procedures. Provide information on roles and responsibilities. This may also include training presented outside of the site.

- **Workshops:** Resemble a seminar but are used to build specific products, such as a draft plan or policy.

PRACTICING

Visual 4.8

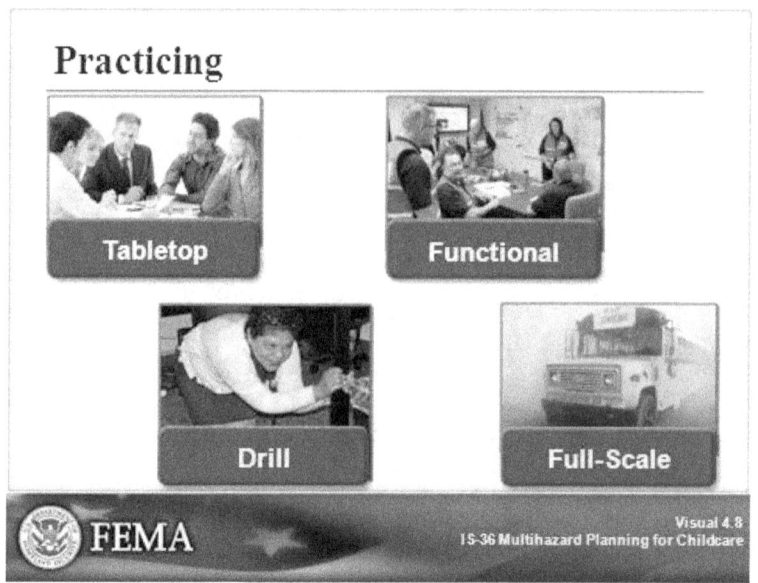

Key Points

Exercises are tools to practice the processes and procedures in your plan. Once you have conducted the necessary training, then you can begin to conduct exercises.

Types of exercises are listed below:

- A **tabletop** is an exercise in which a scenario (often based on actual incidents at the site or recent events in the news) is presented and participants respond as if the scenario were really happening.

- A **drill** is an exercise used to test a single specific operation or function. Drills are often used to test new policies or equipment or practice current skills. Drills can test how well your site responds to simulated emergencies including intruders, fire, or severe weather.

- A **functional exercise** is the simulation of an emergency event that involves site and emergency management personnel "acting out" their actual roles.

- A **full-scale exercise** is a multiagency, multijurisdictional, multidiscipline operations-based exercise involving functional and "boots on the ground" response (e.g., firefighters decontaminating mock victims).

PRACTICING

Visual 4.9

Activity

Instructions: Working in small groups . . .

1. Develop a set of simple instructions for your assigned drill.
2. Be prepared to share your results in 10 minutes.

FEMA

Visual 4.9
IS-36 Multihazard Planning for Childcare

Key Points

Purpose: This activity will give you the opportunity to practice writing and conducting drills.

Instructions: Working in teams:

1. Develop a set of simple instructions for your assigned drill.

2. Be prepared to share your results in 10 minutes.

PRACTICING

Visual 4.10

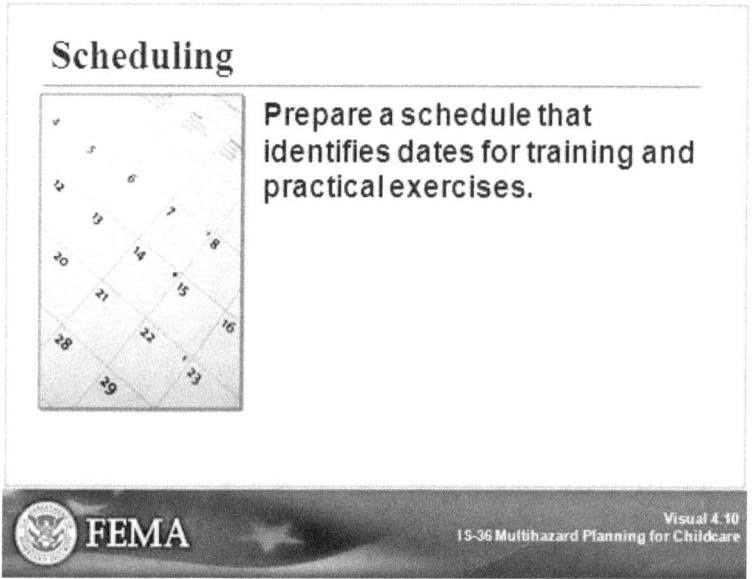

Key Points

Once you have identified the training needs for each audience (staff, children, parents) and how to practice the procedures, the next step is to prepare a schedule that identifies dates for training and practical exercises.

Job Aid: Sample Fire Drill Checklist

Procedure	Good (✓)	Needs Improvement (Specify)
Parents and staff were informed about the drill, in advance.		
Evacuation routes and exits posted.		
Staff knew where to exit.		
Evacuation notification clear.		
911 called (simulate during drill).		
Process to ensure everyone evacuated.		
Staff knew where to gather.		
Children brought to evacuation site.		
Attendance taken before evacuation and at site.		

Job Aid: Sample Evacuation Drill Checklist

Procedure	Good (✓)	Needs Improvement (Specify)
Parents were informed about the drill, in advance.		
Evacuation routes and exits posted.		
Evacuation site communicated to staff.		
Evacuation notification clearly communicated.		
911 called (simulate during drill).		
Emergency kits taken.		
Attendance list taken.		
Staff accounted for children: • Before leaving facility. • In an initial safe location. • At evacuation site.		

MODULE SUMMARY

Visual 4.12

Module Summary

Can you now:

- Describe how you will communicate, train, and practice your preparedness procedures?
- Identify the emergency preparedness information you will share with your community?
- Describe when to update your plan?

FEMA

Visual 4.12
IS-36 Multihazard Planning for Childcare

Key Points

To help you as you prepare to communicate your emergency plan, and to train and practice it at your facility, check out the following resources:

- Resources for communicating with children:
  - Ready Kids: www.ready.gov
  - Sesame Street: Let's Get Ready!: www.sesamestreet.org
  - U.S. Fire Administration for kids: www.usfa.dhs.gov
- Resources for staff and parent training:
  - FEMA independent study courses: www.training.fema.gov/is
  - CERT training: www.citizencorps.gov/cert
- The American Red Cross for first aid training: www.redcross.org
- Resources for family preparedness plans: www.ready.gov

This page intentionally left blank.

MODULE 5: COURSE SUMMARY

MODULE INTRODUCTION

Visual 5.1

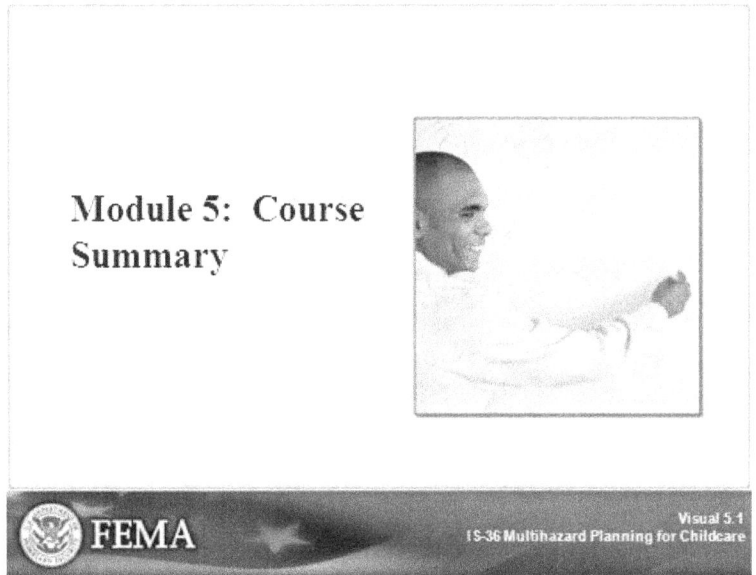

Key Points

This module provides a summary of the course information.

MODULE INTRODUCTION

Visual 5.2

Module Objectives

- Review the steps for developing your emergency plan.
    - Step 1 – Knowing your hazards
    - Step 2 – Developing your plan
    - Step 3 – Testing and updating your plan
- Locate resources to identify what your childcare site needs to do to be prepared.

FEMA
Visual 5.2
IS-36 Multihazard Planning for Childcare

Key Points

By the end of this module, you should be able to:

- Review the steps for developing your emergency plan.
    - Step 1 – Knowing your hazards
    - Step 2 – Developing your plan
    - Step 3 – Testing and updating your plan

- Locate resources to identify what your childcare site needs to do to be prepared.

REVIEW: MODULE 1: COURSE INTRODUCTION

Visual 5.3

Review: Module 1: Course Introduction

- Identifying and addressing hazards.
- Having a plan that addresses evacuating, staying put, and reunification.
- Being able to contact parents/guardians and emergency personnel.
- Establishing relationships with your community stakeholders and including them in your preparedness efforts.
- Preparing your site.

FEMA

Visual 5.3
IS-36 Multihazard Planning for Childcare

Key Points

As a childcare provider, you need to be prepared for emergencies because you care for one of the most vulnerable populations—children.

This responsibility includes:

- Identifying and addressing your hazards and threats.
- Having a plan that addresses evacuating, staying put, and reunification.
- Being able to contact parents/guardians and emergency personnel.
- Establishing relationships with your community stakeholders and including them in your preparedness efforts—planning, reviewing, practicing, and training.
- Preparing your site, which includes conducting activities to lessen the impact of hazards and gathering supplies.

REVIEW: MODULE 2: KNOWING YOUR HAZARDS

Visual 5.4

Review: Module 2: Knowing Your Hazards

- Fires
- General Safety
- Hazardous Materials
- Utility Outages and Blackouts
- Criminal Activity

- Missing, Lost, or Abducted Child
- Severe Weather and Geological Events
- Illness Outbreaks
- Food Safety
- Building and Grounds Hazards

FEMA

Visual 5.4
IS-36 Multihazard Planning for Childcare

Key Points

The first step in the preparedness process is to identify the hazards and threats that you may encounter in your community, and determine those that are of high consequence and most likely. Then you need to address each of the hazards through prevention, mitigation, and preparation.

Common hazards include:

- Fires.
- General safety.
- Hazardous materials and explosions.
- Utility outages and blackouts.
- Criminal activity.
- Missing, lost, or abducted child.
- Severe weather and geological events.
- Illness outbreaks.
- Food safety.
- Building and grounds hazards.

REVIEW: MODULE 3: DEVELOPING PLANS

Visual 5.5

Review: Module 3: Developing Plans

Plan topics:
- Collecting information.
- Posting emergency information.
- Developing procedures for:
  - Sign-in and sign-out.
  - Closing.
  - Shelter-in-place and evacuation.
  - Reunification.
- Preparing emergency kits.
- Accounting for different needs.

Sample Childcare
Emergency Action Plan

FEMA

Visual 5.5
IS-36 Multihazard Planning for Childcare

Key Points

The next step in your preparedness process is to develop a plan with processes and procedures that enable you to be prepared when something does happen.

Whether your site develops a simple emergency action plan or a more complex emergency operations plan, the plan needs to address:

- Collecting information on children in your care.
- Posting emergency information.
- Implementing sign-in and sign-out procedures.
- Establishing closing procedures.
- Developing shelter-in-place and evacuation procedures.
- Knowing how you will reunite children with their parents/guardians.
- Preparing emergency kits.
- Accounting for different needs.

When developing your emergency plan, remember the importance of engaging the whole community.

REVIEW: MODULE 4: TESTING AND UPDATING YOUR PLAN

Visual 5.6

Review: Module 4: Testing and Updating Your Plan

- Communicate the procedures in your plan.
- Conduct and complete training to be prepared for emergencies.
- Conduct drills to practice the procedures in your plan.

FEMA

Visual 5.6
IS-36 Multihazard Planning for Childcare

Key Points

After you have established your plan and procedures, you need to share information with children, staff, volunteers, parents, emergency management officials, and first responders.

- Communicate the procedures in your plan.
- Conduct and complete training to be prepared for emergencies.
- Conduct drills to practice the procedures in your plan.

A plan must not just sit on the shelf. You need to include in your processes how and when you will update the plan, your emergency information, and contact information. These updates will be based on training and exercise results, community input, changes in information, and an analysis of how your plan worked if the plan was implemented when something happened.

NEXT STEPS

Visual 5.7

Key Points

Now that you have completed this course, you have the building blocks to develop and implement an emergency plan to keep everyone at your site safe and:

- Prevent incidents.
- Minimize the impact of hazards.
- Act effectively when something happens.
- Recover quickly.

Once you have developed your plan, remember to test it through training and exercises and keep it updated.

Use the job aid on the following page to review the steps to ensure your childcare site is prepared.

Job Aid: Emergency Plan Checklist

✗	Needs Improvement (Specify)
Knowing Your Hazards: Conduct the following steps to ensure you have addressed your site's high-consequence, most likely hazards and threats.	
	Identify the hazards and threats for your childcare site.
	Identify how to prevent the hazard or threat.
	If the hazard or threat cannot be prevented, identify how to reduce its impact.
	Identify building and grounds mitigation steps.
Developing a Plan: Include the following processes and procedures in your plan, whether it is a simple emergency action plan or a formal emergency operations plan.	
	Develop a process to collect and update information on children at your site.
	Have a process to collect, post, and update emergency contact information.
	Identify procedures to track children's attendance (for example, sign-in/sign-out procedures).
	Identify site closing procedures.
	Designate shelter-in-place procedures.
	Obtain supplies for emergency kits.
	Designate evacuation procedures.
	Include provisions in your procedures for children with access and functional needs.
	Identify parent-child reunification procedures.
	Identify how you will recover from an emergency.
	Document your processes and procedures.
Testing and Updating Your Plan: Communicate about your plan, conduct training and exercises, and provide a process for feedback from your community (e.g., parents/guardians, emergency management officials, first responders, local businesses, and community organizations).	
	Develop relationships within your community (e.g., first responders, emergency management officials, parents/guardians, local businesses and organizations, etc.) and ask for input on your plan.
	Communicate procedures with staff, children, parents/guardians, first responders, emergency management officials, and others.
	Conduct, provide, and complete training as needed.
	Practice your procedures with staff, children, parents, and community participants.
	Have a process for reviewing and updating of your procedures.
	Encourage families and staff to have family emergency preparedness plans.

COURSE SUMMARY

Visual 5.8

Final Exam

Instructions:

1. Take a few moments to review your Student Manual and identify any questions.
2. Make sure that you get all of your questions answered prior to beginning the final test.
3. When taking the test . . .
   - Read each item carefully.
   - Enter the answers online.

FEMA   Visual 5.8
                                                                            IS-36 Multihazard Planning for Childcare

Key Points

1. Take a few moments to review your Student Manual and identify any questions.

2. Make sure that you get all of your questions answered prior to beginning the final test.

3. When taking the test . . .
   - Read each item carefully.
   - Enter the answers online.

You may refer to your Student Manual when completing the test.

To receive a certificate of completion, you must take the 10-question multiple-choice exam and achieve a score of 75%.

Complete your test online and you will receive a certificate of completion in the mail.

- Go to http://training.fema.gov/IS/crslist.asp and click on the link for IS-36.
- Click on "Take Final Exam."

COURSE SUMMARY

Visual 5.9

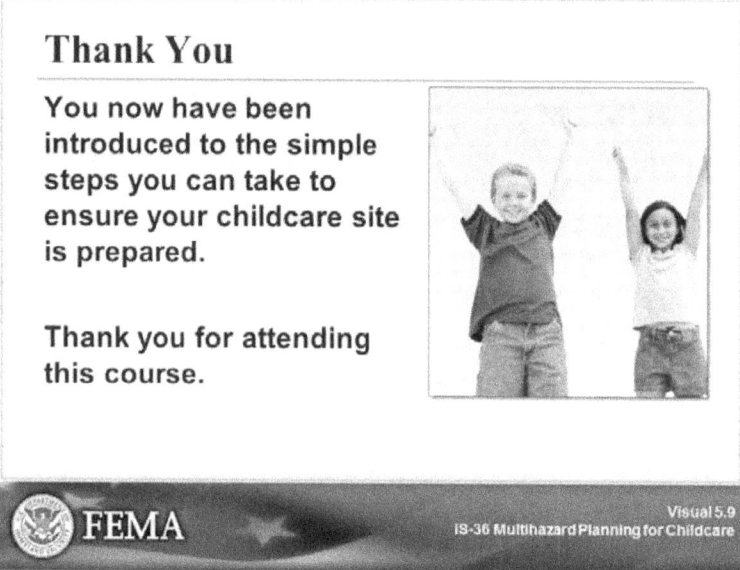

Key Points

Congratulations!

You now have been introduced to the simple steps you can take to ensure your childcare site is prepared.

Thank you for attending this course.